Practical Magic

A WITCHCRAFT SUPPLIES BOOK OF WICCA, SPELLS, AND RUNES

Glenda Blair

© 2019

COPYRIGHT

Practical Magic: A Witchcraft Supplies Book of Wicca, Spells, and Runes

By Glenda Blair

Copyright @2019 By Glenda Blair

All Rights Reserved.

The following eBook is reproduced below with the goal of providing information that is as accurate and as reliable as possible. Regardless, purchasing this eBook can be seen as consent to the fact that both the publisher and the author of this book are in no way experts on the topics discussed within, and that any recommendations or suggestions made herein are for entertainment purposes only. Professionals should be consulted as needed before undertaking any of the action endorsed herein.

This declaration is deemed fair and valid by both the American Bar Association and the Committee of Publishers Association and is legally binding throughout the United States.

Furthermore, the transmission, duplication or reproduction of any of the following work, including precise information, will be considered an illegal act, irrespective whether it is done electronically or in print. The legality extends to creating a secondary or tertiary copy of the work or a recorded copy and is only allowed with express written consent of the Publisher. All additional rights are reserved.

The information in the following pages is broadly considered to be a truthful and accurate account of facts, and as such any inattention, use or misuse of the information in question by the reader will render any resulting actions solely under their purview. There are no scenarios in which the publisher or the original author of this work can be in any fashion deemed liable for any hardship or damages that may befall them after undertaking information described herein.

Additionally, the information found on the following pages is intended for informational purposes only and should thus be considered, universal. As befitting its nature, the information presented is without assurance regarding its continued validity or interim quality. Trademarks that mentioned are done without written consent and can in no way be considered an endorsement from the trademark holder.

Table of Contents

INTRODUCTION 1

    What it Really means to be a Witch 3

CHAPTER 1 - THE HISTORY OF WITCHCRAFT AND HOW IT AFFECTS YOU 7

    Timeline of Wicca and Witchcraft – The path of Persecution to Liberty 12

    The Laws that began Wicca 14

    Important Characters to know in the Craft 33

    The truth about Salem and the Past Persecution of Witches 44

    Collecting the Past Gems and Placing Them into Your Life 46

CHAPTER 2 – THE SEASONS OF THE WHEEL OF THE YEAR 51

    Samhain 54

    Altar Dressings 56

    Crafts and Arts 57

    Yule 64

    Altar Dressings 67

    Crafts and Arts 68

    Imbolc 71

    Altar Dressings 73

    Crafts and Arts 74

    Ostara 78

Altar Dressings 80

Crafts and Arts 81

Beltane 83

Altar Dressings 84

Crafts and Arts 85

Litha 87

Altar Dressings 88

Crafts and Arts 89

Lammas / Lughnasadh 91

Altar Dressings 94

Crafts and Arts 95

Mabon 96

Altar Dressings 98

Crafts and Arts 98

The Path of the Feminine through the Wheel of the Year 103

CHAPTER 3 – FORGING YOUR WITCH-SELF 105

The Wiccan Rede 106

Finding your Witch Name 115

Choosing your name through dreamwork 117

Utilising the plant kingdom for dreamwork 118

Using Numerology to find your Witch name 122

Utilising the method of bag drawing 129

How to Find Your Patron God and Goddess 131

The Altar 136

Sacred Time and Sacred Space 140

Practicing Magick versus Devotion Time 144

THE TOOLS OF THE CRAFT 147

CHAPTER 4 – GRIMOIRE OF CORRESPONDENCES............... 153

GODS, GODDESSES AND SPIRITS TO WORK WITH IN THE BEGINNING
.... 154

OILS, RESINS, INCENSES 160

HERBS, TREES, FLOWERS 163

MAGICKAL TREES.. 164

MAGICKAL FLOWERS 166

COMMON MAGICKAL HERBS 167

CRYSTALS AND STONES... 171

DIVINATION 174

RUNES OF THE ELDER FUTHARK 175

THE TAROT 183

THE BLACK MIRROR.. 192

CRYSTAL BALL GAZING 195

THE LUNAR CALENDAR.. 196

CHAPTER 5 – PATHWORKING'S FOR THE WITCH 203

CHAPTER 6 – USING RITUAL?.. 210

A BASIC STANDARD WICCAN RITUAL.. 210

CIRCLE CASTING DONE BY HIGH PRIESTESS 212

UNIVERSAL INVOCATION 213

THE ELEMENT OF AIR.. 214

THE ELEMENT OF FIRE (S.H) THE ELEMENT OF EARTH (N.H)........ 214

THE ELEMENT OF WATER 215

THE ELEMENT OF EARTH (S.H.) THE ELEMENT OF FIRE (N.H)....... 215

OFFERING LIBATION 217
THE RELEASE OF THE UNIVERSAL SPIRIT 218
DISMISSAL OF THE ELEMENT OF EARTH (S.H) THE ELEMENT OF FIRE (N.H) 219
DISMISSAL OF THE ELEMENT OF WATER.. 219
DISMISSAL OF THE ELEMENT OF FIRE (S.H) THE ELEMENT OF EARTH (N.H) 220
DISMISSAL OF THE ELEMENT OF AIR 220
WHY BUILD ON THE STANDARD WICCAN RITUAL? 221
A NON-WICCAN NORDIC RITUAL WITH PRE-RITUAL TALK AND EXPLANATION 222

CHAPTER 7: SPELL WORK 237

SPELLS FOR LOVE 240
SPELLS FOR ABUNDANCE 245
SPELLS FOR HEALTH AND HEALING AND PROTECTION 249
DRAWING DOWN THE MOON FOR THE SOLITARY PRACTITIONER ... 253
A FINAL WORD OF ADVICE FROM AN OL' WITCH. 257
BIBLIOGRAPHY 259

Introduction

Merry meet and welcome to this humble yet comprehensive guide into the vast landscape of all things Witchcraft. If you have stumbled upon this book, then there is a reason. There is always a reason for everything. Witchcraft teaches us to see these connections and to know what they mean in our lives and in the greater scheme of things. In the core of Witchcraft, which includes Wicca, there is a finite truth that spells how we are all connected to each other, to the plants, the animals, the cosmos. The enlightening path that you have chosen to embark on is one of the most magickal, eye-opening experiences that you will most probably keep for the rest of your life.

It is my hope that you will find your own North-star with the guidance and direction within these pages and that you will always keep your words in order. Within Witchcraft the words that you speak are the most powerful tools that you will ever own. They are the basis for moulding your life and building a strong foundation for magick and forging a solid connection between you and the Divine within and without.

"As above, so below, As within, so without, as the universe, so the soul…"

(Mead, 2017)

WHAT IT REALLY MEANS TO BE A WITCH

Witches are different to the rest of society and yet, they aren't at all. Witches have the same daily lives, are subject to the same changes within governments and social orders and yes, Witches also need to do groceries. Being a Witch does not mean you will be flying your broomstick around town after midnight, it does mean that you will understand and become conscious of your astral body and how to utilise it. Being a Witch does not mean you will be turning your ex-boyfriend into a toad, it does however mean that you will be able to cut cords and soul ties with him and he will cease to affect your life – you could also throw in a *what you sow is what you reap spell.*

Being a Witch means that you will be reading a lot. You will be studying and practicing the arts for the rest of your life. You will make your own life better and you will begin to understand that you cannot help the world, unless you help yourself and fix yourself first. Witchcraft is not for everyone, and that is why there are a bunch of monotheistic religions in place, for those who do need their hand to be held through life.

Witchcraft is a lonely path in society. Witches are given much more freedom today than ever before, but we are still very misunderstood. The path of the Witch is a path of self-discovery, a path of finding and forging your connection to everything around you. Before you can build such a connection you need to traverse the wide landscapes of the self. This journey can take many years and never really comes to an end. Whilst you learn more about yourself, you will learn more about people around you and hopefully come to a place of greater understanding. Witchcraft teaches a great understanding around the necessity of all things. Good and evil are not as they are in the monotheistic religions, each one has a purpose and it is widely understood that if we do not understand the darkness, we can never know the light, and vice versa.

One doesn't become a Witch. One finds the Witch within awakening and the pathway opens up. Books such as this one come to us, we attract people who have great lessons to offer us and stories to tell that will open up new ways of thinking. One of the most important lessons within Witchcraft is that the universal path

– regardless of faith – is a spiral and not a straight ladder. The race is long, and it is only with yourself. You will never be better than anyone else and no one will ever be better than you, or even more important. This path is about you. Being a Witch, is a path for you. If you happen to assist others on your path, then that is wonderful, but you should never attempt to take out your bloated ego on any conversation or instance with another. We are all on this path, learning and assisting where we can. No Witch is stronger or better than another. Yes, many are new to the Craft, but they are also on the path, like you, and sometimes a neophyte's eyes have new insight that can help a High Priestess. It is always important not to judge, always to listen so that you can understand, not so that you can reply, and to keep your own words in good order.

Lastly, being a Witch means that you are a caretaker of the planet, the people who live on it and the spirits that dwell here and beyond the veil. You are a mediator between this world and the next and you have a responsibility to respect and revere the spirit of man, beast and those beyond this space and time. Magick is always to be the last resort. We live a human life and magick can upset the balance of many things, so before you dive into the first spell that catches your eye, learn first to understand the elements, the earth, the cosmos and her inhabitants, and then you will find that magick is as easy as a word, a thought or an idea… and it is not necessary to turn the tides to your will, but to find peace in flowing with the divine will instead.

Chapter 1 - The History of Witchcraft and How it Affects You

The History of Magic by (Levi, 1999) is an excellent book to acquaint you with an all-round history of magic as well as a philosophical take on a worldwide view of magic. Another book that is a literature must-read is the revised edition of The Golden Bough by (Frazer, 1890). Not only do these two works allow you to glimpse into the mindset of magic and folklore but they also gift the reader a time travelling journey into the historical movement of magic.

To grasp the important path of the history of Witchcraft, you need to understand the law of the moon and the law of the sun. The law of both feminine and masculine and how prevalent both are to this day. The law of the moon is what governed the native religions of the past. The people back then were afforded the space and time to delve deep into the feminine mysteries and appreciate the miracles of birth, death and the journey in between. The feminine moon laws govern all the hidden. When man's power and ego driven greed took over, the laws of the sun and masculine strength prevailed. It is from this masculine perspective that the monotheistic or One male God religions were born, and it was faster at conquering whole cities and continents than any feminine path would allow.

The laws of the moon and of the feminine darkness, the shadow path and the reverence of the divine connections was lost to quick hard instant power. Through these monotheistic movements that were born from the order of Pope Constantine 325 A.D., all feminine threats were destroyed. This does not mean that only women were destroyed, it means that all those practicing the 'dark arts' or the arts of anything unknown to the laws of the sun, were destroyed. Persecution happened right across the world. It happened to those that were guilty and those that were not. It became a human excuse to snuff out everything that they did not like or did not understand, and this human trait has not changed much.

Humans want to control, and for this reason, Witchcraft was controlled by packaging it into a beautiful law-abiding religion called Wicca by Freemason and civil servant Gerald Brosseau Gardner in the 1950's. The only Lodge to acknowledge him today is Lodge no. 107, Colombo, Ceylon (Yurkon). This act of his was only possible after the last laws banning Witchcraft in Britain were removed in 1951 through parliamentary action. Gardner worked closely with his ritual architect Doreen Valiente and together they created a Wiccan movement that is stronger today than ever before. To understand why the history of Witchcraft is the way it is, we must understand why humans are the way they are. This process can fill a library, however, in a nutshell we can look at two texts, the first comes from Aradia – Gospel of the Witches by Charles Leland (Leland, 2018) , originally in Italian, this is an excerpt of the voice of the Goddess Diana translated into English:

"And when a priest shall do you injury
By his benedictions, ye shall do to him
Double the harm, and do it in the name
Of me, Diana, Queen of witches all!

And when the priests or the nobility
Shall say to you that you should put your faith
In the Father, Son, and Mary, then reply:
"Your God, the Father, and Maria are
Three devils....

"For the true God the Father is not yours;

For I have come to sweep away the bad,

The men of evil, all will I destroy!"

The second text that we will look at is from the New testament of the Christian bible (Givens, 2008) condemning the children of the abovementioned Goddess to death:

Acts 19:27 – *"So that not only this our craft is in danger to be set to nought; but also, that the temple of the great goddess Diana should be despised, and her magnificence should be destroyed, whom all Asia and the world worshippeth."*

Now to explain the history of Witchcraft and how it affects you, look at the two opposing texts above. Each one is a retaliation of the other or of their own circumstances. Like parliament, one party fights against another for dominance. Just so the faiths of the history of mankind wrote pieces and feigned the words of Gods to stir the minds of the people. Does this mean that all texts are not the words of God/s? Absolutely not, I do believe that there are many that are God-inspired and many that have the best intention of their specific people in mind but that is as far as it gets.

Witchcraft's history is viciously ugly, especially the Würzburg Witch Trials in Germany (Roper). We must understand though that this is the human condition and not the work of religions or a reflection of people currently in those religions. One of the greatest displays of human evolution will be when we do not cut things in two opposing forces. Good versus evil occurs in every human creation. All the myths and all the faith-based texts. Someone must always be the devil.

How does it affect you? It doesn't. The history of Witchcraft must be taken with a bucket of salt when learning the recipes, spells and methods, but as far as being a subject in the past, you are not. You are a Witch in the 21st Century, possibly a millennial and that means that you do not need to bear the burden of the past, because Witchcraft is not its past, it is a path inward to assist outward and that means that you are only subject to your own actions and reactions.

Mass genocide across the timeline of what we believe to be Witchcraft would be more equated to people's fear of the unknown and the laws that came into effect have simply been rewritten, regurgitated and reinforced over and over again. To be a Witch means that you are to keep your life in better order than the next person so that you never give away an opportunity to have a feared finger pointed at you.

Timeline of Wicca and Witchcraft – The Path of Persecution to Liberty

This timeline serves to outline the most important and pivotal points in what made Witchcraft what it is today, as well as what caused the laws that persecuted those of the past and present to be formed.

- 3rd Millennium BC - Cuneiform Law – A concise set of laws that are thought to be the beginning of crazed laws against what was seen as unfit action as well as against those practicing Witchcraft.

- 1700 BC – The Code of Hammurabi – The first instance where extreme punishment against a person found guilty of practicing Witchcraft is mentioned.

- 15th Century BC – Torah – Written with the Babylonian Laws in mind, the Torah mentions approximately five excerpts where Witchcraft is banned, sometimes punishable by death.

- 1860 – Eliphas Levi begins to write Histoire de la Magie or History of Magic.

- 1888 – Helena Petrovna Blavatsky founds The Theosophical Publishing Company and publishes the first edition of The Secret Doctrine.

- 1907 – Aleister Crowley and George Cecil Jones form the esoteric Order entitled A.-.A.-.

- Witchcraft Act of 1542 – One of the first modern world laws to be passed and render Witchcraft punishable by death.

- 1911 – Arthur Edward Waite published the Pictorial Key to the Tarot; he is also the co-creator of the Rider-Waite Tarot Deck.

- 1920 – Paul Foster Case publishes his first work on the occult in An Introduction to the Study of the Tarot.

- 1921 – Margaret Alice Murray publishes her Witchcraft findings with great success in her book The Witch-cult in Western Europe.

- 26 September 1944 – Jane Rebecca Yorke is convicted of *"pretending to cause the spirits of deceased persons to be present"* She is the last documented victim of the Witchcraft Acts in the British Isles.

- 1936 – Dion Fortune publishes her second Occult novel, The Goat-foot God.

- 1939 – Gerald Brosseau Gardner is initiated into the New Forest Coven.

- 1948 – Robert Graves publishes The White Goddess.

- 1949 – Gerald Brosseau Gardner publishes his Witchcraft findings in High Magic's Aid.

- 1951 – The Witchcraft Act of 1542 is finally repealed.

- 1954 – Gerald Brosseau Gardner publishes Witchcraft Today.

- 1957 – Doreen Valiente leaves Gardner's coven.

- 1957 – The Parliament of South Africa instates The Witchcraft Suppression Act of 1957, this law stands to this day in the country, however it is not enforced as strongly as in the past.

- 1959 – Gerald Brosseau Gardner founds the Bricket Wood Coven and forms the lineage that is known today as Gardnerian Wicca.

- 1960's – Raymond Howard founds the Coven of Atho.

- 1965 – Alex and Maxine Sanders form what is known today as Alexandrian Wicca.

- 1970's – Dianic Wicca, a Goddess worshipping form of Wicca is formed by Zsuzsanna Budapest.

- 1981 – Stewart and Janet Farrar, both authors, write a series of books that become the core point in many covens and pagan circles today. The books include but are not limited to: The Witches Bible (1996), The Witches God (1989), The Witches Goddess (1987).

THE LAWS THAT BEGAN WICCA

The 161 Laws of Gerald Brosseau Gardner (Gardner, 2009)

1. The Law was made and ordained of old.

2. The Law was made for the Wicca, to advise and help in their troubles.

3. The Wicca should give due worship to the gods and obey their will, which they ordain, for it was made for the good of Wicca as the

worship of the Wicca is good for the gods. For the gods love the brethren of Wicca.

4. As a man loveth a woman by mastering her.

5. So the Wicca should love the gods by being mastered by them.

6. And it is necessary that the Circle, which is the temple of the gods, should be truly cast and purified. And that it may be a fit place for the gods to enter.

7. And the Wicca shall be properly prepared and purified to enter the presence of the gods.

8. With love and worship in their hearts, they shall raise power from their bodies to give power to the gods.

9. As has been taught of old.

10. For in this way only may men have communion with the gods, for the gods cannot help man without the help of man.

11. And the High Priestess shall rule her coven as the representative of the God.

12. And the High Priest shall support her as the representative of the God.

13. And the High Priestess shall choose whom she will, be he of sufficient rank, to be her High Priest.

14. For as the god himself kissed her feet in the fivefold salute, laying his power at the feet of the Goddess because of her youth and beauty, her sweetness and kindness, her wisdom and justice, her humility and generosity,

15. So he resigned all his power to her.

16. But the High Priestess should ever mind that all power comes from him.

17. It is only lent, to be used wisely and justly.

18. And the greatest virtue of a High priestess be that she recognizes that youth is necessary to the representative of the goddess.

19. So she will gracefully retire in favor of a younger woman should the Coven so decide in council.

20. For a true High Priestess realizes that gracefully surrendering pride of place is one of the greatest virtues.

21. And that thereby she will return to that pride of place in another life, with greater power and beauty.

22. In the old days, when witchdom extended far, we were free and worshipped in all the greater temples.

23. But in these unhappy times we must celebrate our sacred mysteries in secret.

24. So be it ordained, that none but the Wicca may see our mysteries, for our enemies are many and torture loosens the tongue of man.

25. So be it ordained that no Coven shall know where the next Coven bide.

26. Or who its members be, save only the Priest and Priestess and messenger.

27. And there shall be no communication between them, save by the messenger of the gods, or the summoner.

28. And only if it be safe may the covens meet in some safe place for the great festivals.

29. And while there, none shall say whence they came nor give their true names.

30. To this end, any that are tortured in their agony may not tell if they do not know.

31. So be it ordained that no one shall tell anyone not of the craft who be of the Wicca, nor give any names or where they bide, or in any way tell anything which can betray any of us to our foes.

32. Nor may he tell where the Covendom be.

33. Or the Coven stead.

34. Or where the meetings be.

35. And if any break these laws, even under torture, THE CURSE OF THE GODDESS SHALL BE UPON THEM, so they may never be reborn on earth and may remain where they belong, in the hell of the Christians.

36. Let each High Priestess govern her Coven with justice and love, with the help and advice of the High Priest and the Elders, always heeding the advice of the messenger of the gods if he cometh.

37. She will heed all complains of all Brothers and strive to settle all differences among them.

38. But it must be recognized that there will always be people who will ever strive to force others to do as they will.

39. These are not necessarily evil.

40. And they oft have good ideas and such ideas should be talked over in council.

41. But if they will not agree with their Brothers, or if they say,

42. "I will not work under this High Priestess,"

43. It hath ever been the Old Law to be convenient to the Brethren and to avoid disputes.

44. Any of the third may claim to find a new Coven because they live over a league away from the Coven stead, or that they are about to do so.

45. Anyone living within the Covendom and wishing to form a new Coven shall tell the Elders of their intention and on the instant avoid their dwelling and remove to the new Covendom.

46. Members of the old Coven may join the new one when it is formed. But if they do, they must utterly avoid the old Coven.

47. The Elders of the new and the old Covens should meet in peace and brotherly love to decide the new boundaries.

48. Those of the craft who dwell outside both Covendoms may join either but not both.

49. Though all may, if the Elders agree, meet for the great festivals if it be truly in peace and brotherly love,

50. But splitting the Coven off means strife, so for this reason these Laws were made of old and may the CURSE OF THE GODDESS BE ON ANY WHO DISREGARD THEM. So be it ordained.

51. If you would keep a book, let it be in your own hand of write. Let brothers and sisters copy what they will, but never let the book out of your hands, and never keep the writings of another.

52. For if it be found in their hand of write, they may be taken and arraigned. Let each guard his own writings and destroy them

53. whenever danger threatens.

54. Learn as much as you may by heart and, when danger is past, rewrite your book, and it be safe.

55. For this reason, if any die, destroy their book if they have not been able to.

56. For, if it be found, 'tis clear proof against them.

57. And our oppressors know well "Ye may not be a witch alone".

58. So all their kin and friends be in danger of torture.

59. So destroy everything not necessary.

60. If your book be found on you, 'tis clear proof against you alone, you may be arraigned.

61. Keep all thoughts of the craft from your mind.

62. If the torture be too great to bear, say, "I will confess. I can't bear this torture. What do you want me to say?"

63. If they try to make you speak of the Brotherhood, do not.

64. But if they try to make you speak of impossibilities such as flying through the air, consorting with a Christian devil or sacrificing children, or eating men's flesh.

65. To obtain relief from torture say, "I had an evil dream I was beside myself; I was crazed."

66. Not all magistrates are bad, if there be an excuse, they may show mercy.

67. If you have confessed ought, deny it afterwards, say you babbled under torture, and say you knew not what you said.

68. If you are condemned, fear not.

69. The Brotherhood is powerful and will help you to escape if you stand steadfast, but if you betray ought there is no hope for you in this life or in that to come.

70. Be sure, if steadfast you go to the pyre, drugs will reach you, you will feel naught you go to death and what lies beyond, the ecstasy of the goddess.

71. To avoid discovery, let the working tools be as ordinary things that any may have in their houses.

72. Let the pentacles be of wax so that they may be broken at once or melted.

73. Have no sword unless your rank allows it.

74. Have no names or signs on anything.

75. Write the names and signs on them in ink before consecrating them and wash it off immediately afterwards.

76. Let the color of the hilts tell which is which.

77. Do not engrave them unless they cause discovery.

78. Ever remember ye are the hidden children of the Goddess so never do anything to disgrace them or Her.

79. Never boast, never threaten, never say you would wish ill of anyone.

80. If any person not in the Circle, speak of the craft, say, "Speak not to me of such, it frightens me, 'tis evil luck to speak of it.

81. For this reason, the Christians have their spies everywhere. These speak as if they were well affected to us, as if they wouldn't come into our meetings, saying, "My mother used to worship the Old Ones. I would I could go myself."

82. To such as these ever deny all knowledge.

83. But to others, ever say, "Tis foolish men talk of witches flying through the air. To do so they must be as light as thistledown. And

men say that witches all be blear eyed old crones, so what pleasure can there be at a witch meeting such as folks talk on?"

84. And say, "Many wise men now say there be no such creatures."

85. Ever make it a jest, and in some future time perhaps, the persecution may die and we may worship our gods in safety again.

86. Let us all pray for that happy day.

87. May the blessings of the Goddess and God be on all who keep these Laws which are ordained.

88. If the craft hath any appendage, let all guard it and witchcraft in the land," because our oppressors of old make it heresy not to believe in witchcraft and so a crime to deny it which thereby puts you under suspicion.

89. And let all justly guard all monies of the craft.

90. And if any Brother truly wrought it, `tis right they have their pay, and it be just. And this be not taking money for the art, but for good and honest work.

91. And even the Christians say, "The laborer is worthy of his hire," but if any Brother work willingly for the good of the craft without pay, `tis but to their greater honor. So be it ordained.

92. If there be any dispute or quarrel among the Brethren, the High Priestess shall straightly convene the Elders and enquire into the matter, and they shall hear both sides, first alone and then together.

93. And they shall decide justly, not favoring one side or the other.

94. Ever recognizing there be people who can never agree to work under others.

95. But at the same time; there be some people who cannot rule justly.

96. To those who ever must be chief, there is one answer.

97. Void the Coven or seek another one, or make a Coven of your own, taking with you those who will go.

98. To those who cannot, justly the answer be, "Those who cannot bear your rule will leave with you.

99. For none may come to meetings with those whom they are at variance.

100. So, an either cannot agree, get hence, for the craft must ever survive, so be it ordained.

101. In the olden days when we had power, we could use the art against any who illtreated the Brotherhood. But in these evil days we must not do so. For our enemies have devised a burning pit of

everlasting fire into which they say their god casteth all the people who worship him, except it be the very few who are released by their priests, spells and masses. And this be chiefly by giving monies and rich gifts to receive his favor for their great god is ever in need of money.

102. But as our gods need our aid to make fertility for man and crops, so is the god of the Christians ever in need of man's help to search out and destroy us. Their priests ever tell them that any who get our help are damned to this hell forever, so men be mad with the terror of it.

103. But they make men believe that they may escape this hell if they give victims to the tormentors. So for this reason all be forever spying, thinking, "And I can catch but one of these Wicca, I will escape from this fiery pit."

104. So for this reason we have our hides, and men searching long and Doth finding, say, "There be none, or if there be, they be in a far country."

105. But when one of our oppressors die, or even be sick, ever is the cry, "This be witches' malice", and the hunt is up again. And though they slay ten of their own to one of ours, still they care not. They have countless thousands.

106. While we are few indeed. So be it ordained.

107. That none shall use the art in any way to do ill to any.

108. However much they injure us, harm none. And now times many believe we exist not.

109. That this Law shall ever continue to help us in our plight, no one, however great an injury or injustice they receive, may use the art in any way to do ill, or harm any. But they may, after great consultations with all, use the art to restrain Christians from harming us Brothers, but only to constrain them and never to punish.

110. To this end men will say, "Such a one is a mighty searcher out, and a persecutor of old women when they desire to be witches, and none hath done him harm, so it be proof that they cannot or more truly there be none.

111. For all know full well that so many folk have died because someone had a grudge against them, or were persecuted because they had money or goods to seize, or because they had none to bribe the searchers. And many have died because they were scolding old women. So much that men now say that only old women are witches.

112. And this be to our advantage and turns suspicion away from us.

113. In England and Scotland 'tis now many a year since a witch hath died the death. But any misuse of the power might raise the persecution again.

114. So never break this Law, however much you are tempted, and never consent to its being broken in the least.

115. If you know it is being broken, you must work strongly against it.

116. And any High Priestess or High Priest who consents to its breach must immediately be deposed for tis the blood of the Brethren they endanger.

117. Do good, and it be safe, and only if it be safe.

118. And strictly keep to the Old Law.

119. Never accept money for the work of the art, for money ever smeareth the taker. "Tis sorcerers and conjurors and the priests of the Christians who ever accept money for the use of their arts. And they sell pardons to let men escape from their sins.

120. Be not as these. If you accept no money, you will be free from temptation to use the art for evil causes.

121. All may use the art for their own advantage or for the advantage of the craft only if you are sure you harm none.

122. But ever let the Coven debate this at length. Only if all are satisfied that none may be harmed, may the art be used.

123. If it is not possible to achieve your ends one way, perchance the aim may be achieved by acting in a different way so as to harm none. MAY THE CURSE OF THE GODDESS BE UPON ANY WHO BREAKETH THIS LAW. So be it ordained.

124. "Tis judged lawful if ever any of the craft need a house or land and none will sell, to incline the owner's mind so as to be willing to sell, provided it harmeth him not in any way and the full price is paid without haggling.

125. Never bargain or cheapen anything whilst you buy by the art. So be it ordained.

126. Tis the Old Law and the most important of all laws, that no one may do anything which will endanger any of the craft, or bring them into contact with the law of the land or any persecutors

127. In any dispute between the Brethren, no one may invoke any laws but those of the craft.

128. Or any tribunal but that of the Priestess, Priest and Elders.

129. It is not forbidden to say as Christians do, "There be witchcraft in the land," because our oppressors of old make it heresy not to

believe in witchcraft and so a crime to deny it which thereby puts you under suspicion.

130. But ever say, "I know not of it here, perchance there may be but afar off, I know not where."

131. But ever speak of them as old crones, consorting with the devil and riding through the air.

132. And ever say, "But how may many ride the air if they be not as light as thistledown."

133. But the curse of the Goddess be on any who cast suspicion on any of the Brotherhood.

134. Or who speak of any real meeting place or where they bide.

135. Let the craft keep books with the names of all herbs which are good, and all cures so all may learn.

136. But keep another book with all Bills and Apices and let only the Elders and other trustworthy people have this knowledge. So be it ordained.

137. And may the blessings of the gods be on all who keep these Laws, and the curses of both the God and the Goddess be on all who break them.

138. Remember the art is the secret of the gods and may only be used in earnest and never for show or vain glory.

139. Magicians and Christians may taunt us saying, "You have no power, show us your power. Do magic before our eyes, then only will we believe," seeking to cause us to betray the art before them.

140. Heed them not, for the art is holy and may only be used in need, and the curse of the gods be on any who break this Law.

141. It ever be the way with women and with men also, that they ever seek new love. 142. Nor should we reprove them for this.

143. But it may be found a disadvantage to the craft.

144. And so many a time it has happened that a High Priest or a High Priestess, impelled by love, hath departed with their love. That is, they have left the Coven.

145. Now if the High Priestess wishes to resign, she may do so in full Coven.

146. And this resignation is valid.

147. But if they should run off without resigning, who may know if they may not return in a few months?

148. So the Law is, if a High Priestess leaves her Coven, she be taken back and all be as before.

149. Meanwhile, if she has a deputy, that deputy shall act as High Priestess for as long as the High Priestess is away.

150. If she returns not at the end of a year and a day, then shall the Coven elect a new High Priestess. 151. Unless there is a good reason to the contrary.

152. The person who has done the work shall reap the benefit of the reward, maiden and deputy of the High Priestess.

153. It had been found that practicing the art doth cause a fondness between aspirant and tutor, and it is the cause of better results if this be so.

154. And if for any reason this be undesirable, it can easily be avoided by both persons from the outset firmly resolving in their minds to be as brother and sister, or parent and child.

155. And it is for this reason that a man may be taught only by a woman and a woman by a man, and women and women should not attempt these practices together. So be it ordained.

156. Order and discipline must be kept.

157. A High Priestess or a High Priest may, and should, punish all faults.

158. To this end all fault and his sentence pronounced.

159. All properly prepared, the culprit should be told his fault, and his sentence pronounced.

160. Punishment should be followed by something amusing.

161. The culprit must acknowledge the justice of the punishment by kissing the hand on receiving sentence and again thanking for punishment received. So be it ordained."

IMPORTANT CHARACTERS TO KNOW IN THE

CRAFT

There are thousands of individuals who dedicated their lives to the pursuit of Occult knowledge. Their pursuits and the historical markings of their publications are what moulded Witchcraft and Wicca into everything that it is today. It is important to understand that each one of these people and each one of the markings throughout our history are simply the findings of personal experiences and a subjective action based on the time and place that each one of them found themselves.

Witchcraft was and is still a relationship with the divine that is found within oneself and in the world around us. A witch living in the forest will have a vastly different approach to on living in the hustle and bustle of the city. For this reason, it is imperative to research and avidly read all the notable minds that formed Witchcraft today, but also to understand that their methods and their ways of approaching the divine may or may not be the same as yours.

Arthur Edward Waite

An initiate in the Golden Dawn as well as a Freemason, initiated 19th September 1901, A. E. Waite is the co-creator of the Rider-Waite Tarot Deck, he was also an author and dedicated much of his occult knowledge into creating the Tarot deck that almost all other Tarot decks are forged from.

Aleister Crowley

Dubbed 'The Beast of Man', Aleister Crowley seemed to delight in shock and horror. He also dedicated his life, in between the urge of needing to be accepted, to the study of the Occult and finding that one thing that would prove the existence of the worlds beyond the veil.

Eliphas Levi

French born; Levi was known as 'The Last Magi'. A 33rd degree Freemason. His work in A History of Magic and The Doctrine of Transcendental Magic are sometimes referred to as the most detailed important works to mark the Witchcraft movement and minds behind the Wiccan religion.

Helena Petrovna Blavatsky

Blavatsky set the stage with her works entitled Isis Unveiled and The Secret Doctrine. Even though the works are extensive reading, she reaches into the core of the philosophical soul and gifts practitioners and excellent platform to understand their own path.

Zsuzsanna Emese Mokcsay (Budapest)

The Hungarian born founder of Dianic Wicca, author and activist helped to shape the world of Wicca and Witchcraft. She is perhaps solely responsible for setting the stage and tipping the scale for future authors and practitioners of the Goddess worshipping movements within Wicca and occult circles.

Doreen Valiente

Doreen Valiente was the chief ritual architect and right hand to Gerald Gardner. The works that she produced are still used today in many, if not all first- and second-degree manuals of Wiccan circles. She devised the softer and more devotional side to the Freemason influence that Gardner brought to the table. It is said that without her incredible influence, Wicca would not be what it is today.

Gerald Brosseau Gardner

Known as The Father of Modern Wicca, Gerald was a Freemason and much of his work has been speculated to be the culmination of a vast imagination and the experience of a Freemason. His bold move to publish works and form The Bricket Wood Coven at the time when he did are one of the most pivotal movements toward the liberation and world acceptance of Witchcraft today.

Scott Cunningham

Originally born, Scott Douglas Cunningham, received his training under Raven Grimassi. He managed to publish several books on Wicca and Witchcraft and his book *Wicca: A guide for the solitary practitioner* is one of the most well-known book on Wicca as well as remaining the most successfully sold book on the subject, worldwide.

Raymond Buckland

For the solitary practitioners and the coven practitioners, Raymond Buckland's work opened many doors that were previously not even dared to be opened. Raymond Buckland was initiated by Gerald Brosseau Gardner himself and he is the founder of Seax Wicca. Seax Wicca is a tradition of Wicca that does not frown upon self-initiation and actually encourages it.

THE TRUTH ABOUT SALEM AND THE PAST

PERSECUTION OF WITCHES

Salem is one of the hottest places to find Witchcraft merchandise today. The entire town vibrates with a history that has nothing to do with Witchcraft. The American History of Witchcraft has almost nothing to do with Witchcraft on its own. The Salem Colony that attests to be the place where Witches were burned at the stake is a false claim. The colony was under British rule in 1692 and the entire Salem trial by hanging was a family feud that led to a mass hysteria which could not be proven to relate to Witchcraft at all.

One of the most violent and vicious occurrences of mass murders due to the suspicion of Witchcraft was the Würzburg Witch Trials in Germany. At these trials a total of 900 people were found to be guilty. The children who were put to death were accused of having sexual relations with the devil. Over and above those atrocities, it is said that of the 900 people, 19 of them were Catholic Priests. The others that almost top these are the Bamberg, The Trier, and The Fulda Witch Trials. Salem, however famous has no Witchcraft standing according to scholarly accounts.

It has become customary within many Wiccan circles across the world to be a descendant of a Witch who was burned at the stake in Salem. It has also become an important chip on the shoulder to announce the fact that you come from a long line of Witches. None of that matters in this present day where we find ourselves. Witchcraft is not about the past at all. It is about you and your relationship to those people around you. It is about your relationship to the Divine. It is about your own set of morals and how you do at keeping your word of honour. What can you take from Salem? A good excursion, a journey into a modern Witches town, but that is all. The history needs to be made by you.

COLLECTING THE PAST GEMS AND PLACING THEM INTO YOUR LIFE

To collect information from the past, we need to first understand who and what we are now. The present day is what counts. As a Witch, your magick can only work if you know what and who you are. It is important to take heed of the writings, successes and grave errors of past influencers within the Witchcraft landscape. There are always two ways of learning: The first is through your own failing and falling and the second is through the mistakes of others. For this reason, it is important to read and study as much as you can, but always keep the scales tipped more toward your own experience and remember to record everything.

Ritual within Witchcraft, and Wicca more specifically, works. Therefore, we use it throughout the year and throughout our magickal path. If, for some reason you find that changing a certain thing works for you, then do so. There must never be fear in Witchcraft as fear is without a doubt the mind and magick killer. Make your path your own. Take what you need from the past lore and mould it into your own path. Witchcraft will never hold your hand or lead you; it is you who lead the way.

Each Witch has his/her own set of laws, rules, guidelines and magick secrets, spells, potions and ways of doing things. There is no right and no wrong when formulating your own path. It is important to collect things and incorporate things into what suits your personality. One of the most important questions to ask when choosing to absorb new information into your collection is:

"Does this addition of information bring me closer to the divine spirit within me and without me?"

Witchcraft is not about gaining power over others. Ego driven pursuits of knowledge are never a good idea. They do not get one anywhere and in the greater scheme of things, there really is no power over another without the consequence of death. It is wise to feel your way around the landscape of Witchcraft, both in its past and in its present-day form. When reading someone else's work, whether they be a witch or not, make sure that the information resonates with your soul. If it does not resonate, leave it to be. Do not feel guilty about not enjoying a piece of work that is classified as an important piece of literature by other witches or Wiccans. Your intuition must guide you and it is true that one person's truth is another man's downfall.

Many neophytes begin asking questions such as:

"Where do I begin?", "There is so much information, I don't know if I can read everything and I do not know even which book is right and which one is not."

The other part that comes with these questions is the mad frenzy that new Witches find themselves in. They want every crystal, every book, every form of divination and they spend all their hard-earned money on everything that they can lay their hands on. This is something that happens to every single one of us. The reason behind it is simple. You have found a path that you wish that you had found earlier in life and so now you are making up for the lost time. If this sounds like you then please just breathe. Breathe in, go sit on the grass outside and feel mother nature. Go and absorb her essence and calm yourself into the knowledge that you are enough. You do not need the thousands of crystals and books and goodies to learn. You do need to learn about what makes you happy from the inside. You can only learn that by being calm about the process.

Understand that you will be drawn by your intuition to what you are destined to learn. Some witches, for example, never learn the tarot, but they are excellent at using the pendulum or at dowsing. Many books will say that to be a witch you need to be able to use the tarot; you need to wear black; you need to speak to the dead etc. This is absolute rubbish. Witchcraft is not a pretty little black box that all of us climb into and learn the tarot whilst speaking to the dead. Everyone is unique and there are no two witches that are alike.

When you take your gems from the past and the present, make sure that they mirror who you are. Yes, you will grow out of some of them, but if the information that you are collecting resonates with who you are then you will never forget it. There is really no point in throwing out your wardrobe, replacing it with all black clothes, if pink or baby blue is really your colour. Similarly, there is no point in spending thousands on buying new tarot decks because you can't find one that resonates with your soul, and meanwhile you are meant to be reading Lenormand. It is imperative that you take this path slowly and with much consideration on the choices that you make.

At the end of the day, all that matters are the relationships that you keep with your own divinity. Witchcraft is the path of the witch, it is his/her path alone, no one else's. Besides, we all enter and leave this world with the thoughts and souls that we alone have nurtured. Why is life then so different?

Chapter 2 – The Seasons of the Wheel of the Year

The Wheel of the Year is not only a storyline about understanding the seasonal changes and how the earth and her creatures are affected, it is also the storyline of the deep psychological processes that we as humans undergo through this continuous cycle. The Wiccan Wheel of the Year is a union between Celtic and Germanic lore devised by Gerald Brosseau Gardner. He sought to include both the solstices and the equinoxes to give practitioners a full eight-spoke wheel of the year to celebrate and understand the seasonal changes of our great mother earth.

There are many stories that find themselves intertwined with the Wiccan wheel of the year. It is often an extreme confusion for people when they hear the stories of the wheel of the year and cannot understand the discrepancies in it. There are no discrepancies in the wheel of the year, there are however two prominent cultures gifting their understanding of the seasons and that is why we often hear people explain how the wheel of the year makes no sense.

It is also extremely common for practitioners of the craft to have absolutely no idea about the wheel of the year and what each festival stands for. Social media has made it easy to remember these pivotal points of change because as soon as one person says *"Merry Yule"* it is shared, and the word is passed on. There is a great difference between northern and southern hemisphere worship. Not only does the wheel of the year swop around but so does circle casting, ritual procession and the placement of the various elemental guardians.

How do you know what to practice and when? Well, observe the world around you. The solstices and the equinoxes find themselves in the heart of the season or at its apex. In other words, Samhain is in found to be celebrated in the heart or in the zenith of Fall / Autumn. Similarly, Yule is found to be in the heart of Winter as well as being on the longest night and the shortest day. We need to understand the world around us to be able to live, love and incorporate the wheel of the year into our everyday lives.

The practice of celebrating the seasonal changes is probably the most important work that you can do in becoming and remaining a witch. A witch knows her seasons, he/she knows the first bud of spring well, and many have collected these first leaves or buds to use in powerful life changing magick. A witch knows when it is the time of the thinning of the veil and he/she naturally prepare for his/her new year. It is this continual cycle, this spiral of continuation that provides the witch with the knowledge of how to bring the rains to fall when the weatherman did not predict them for another week. It is this incredible ongoing cycle of the seasons that allow witches to understand their own inner makeup and to prepare, heal and change their lives as they see fit. If you are deciding on what to do, where to start or how you can become a better witch, then make sure to learn your wheel of the year, and always record your dates, your observations and your activities, no matter how small or how big.

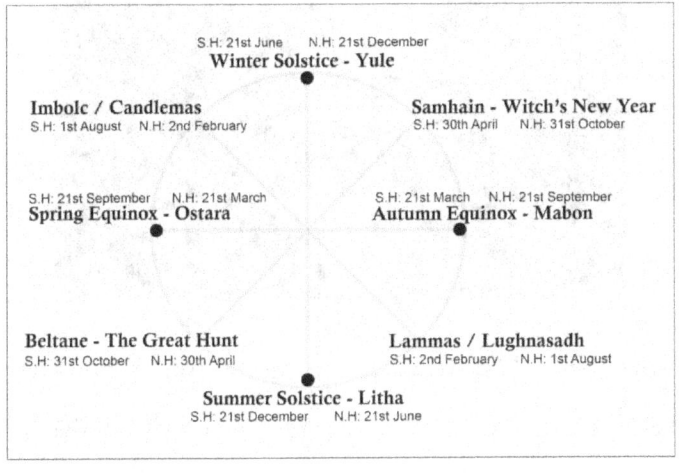

Samhain

Happy New Year Witches! Welcome to the time when the veil is at its thinnest. A night without the gods, and a festival of the dead. Samhain is the night of dining with the ancestors and experiencing the spirit world in your own home. This is one of the most important celebrations in Witchcraft, not because it is full of spirits or of skulls, pumpkins and so forth, but because it is the one time in the year where we can hear ourselves think.

Samhain is full of introspection. As the dark twin of Beltane, Samhain is a quiet festival of introspection, communing with those that have passed on into the Summerland's and of being with the spirit world. Sadly, the Christian influence brought about Halloween, or All Hallows Eve, but despite the mockery, we now get to practice Samhain without being thought of as creepy or dangerous.

During Samhain, both the God and Goddess are wading through the perils of the underworld. They too are undergoing great change and as a result, they are not placed on the altar as Wiccan deities. It is customary however, to invoke, not only evoke an underworld deity at this time to deliver messages to the coven or to the people present. Please do not even attempt an invocation if you are not sure what you are doing. Evocation is a lot safer and always, always cast circle before doing any sort of work with the spirits or with deity.

Not only is Samhain a time for the ancestors but it is also a time that we rest and rethink our lives. This is a time to throw out the old and think about what we would like in our lives instead. It is customary to do rituals of cord cutting and of banishing old habits. This is where we take off the old dusty rags and await the wheels turning to prepare, plan and create the new ones.

ALTAR DRESSINGS

- Reds, browns, oranges and black coloured cloths and drapes
- Ancestral imagery and items of the persons
- Black mirrors
- Skulls
- Black candles
- White candles
- Red Candles
- Pumpkins
- Twigs
- Underworld representations
- Dark hooded figures
- Crystal balls
- Tarot decks
- Myrrh & Patchouli
- Witches Ladders

CRAFTS AND ARTS

Broom Making

Samhain is the best time to be making a new broom. Last year's broom can be used in the fire to represent cleansing out the old and making room for the new. How would you begin such a task?

What you will need:

- Twigs / old branches / Grass
- A long branch that has fallen from a magickal tree such as willow or oak
- Strong cotton
- Copper jewellery wire (Optional)
- A bowl of sea salt

- A bottle of mineral water
- A white candle
- Incense of your choice and the holder so as not to burn the floor
- Paint (optional)
- Ribbon of your choice
- Decorating items such as glitter glue or charms

Firstly, the broom is used for cleansing the energy of the desired space. It is not used to sweep and should be kept as a magickal item at all times. Begin the process by casting a nice big circle and remember to keep all your items inside the circle, unless you are knowledgeable about cutting doorways in the circle to go and fetch the goodies that you have forgotten.

Begin by blessing the salt:

"Oh, creature of earth, I cleanse, consecrate and bless thee, you are now fit to dwell in sacred space."

Bless the water:

"Oh, creature of Water, I cleanse, consecrate and bless thee, you are now fit to dwell in sacred space."

Now add the salt to the water and stir with your athame if you have one, or with your index finger, both work exactly the same. As you are stirring, repeat the following words:

"Holy Water and Holy Earth combined to work as one single power – to cleanse, to purify, to bless and to charge as I see fit. As I will, so mote it be."

When you completed this, you have in fact made holy water. This water can be further strengthened by adding essential oils if you would like but this is not necessary. Now light your candle and sweep your hand over the flame repeating:

"Oh, creature of fire, I cleanse, consecrate and bless thee, you are now fit to dwell in sacred space."

Light the incense and sweep your hand through the smoke and repeat:

"Oh, creature of Air, I cleanse, consecrate and bless thee, you are now fit to dwell in sacred space."

Now we can begin to build our broom. Lay your branch or long stick in front of you. Take the twigs / dry branches / grass and lay them down with the stick in the centre of the bunch. Take the copper wire and bound the twigs / dry branches or grass as tight as you can to the branch. You must do this in three places. If you do not have copper wire at hand, then strong cotton or embroidery cotton will work as well. Once you have done this, take your ribbon and go over the areas where you have tied the broom. Now paint and decorate your broom as you see fit.

When your broom is done, lay it in front of you and place the holy water, candle and incense in front of the broom. Now allow the broom to be cleansed, consecrated, blessed and charged with your energy and the energy of the elements. Pass the broom through the fire of the candle, just do not set it alight. Whilst doing this repeat:

"This broom, this tool of the craft

born from my hands and born from my heart,

I pass it through Fire to cleanse, to charge and to bless,

This broom is now a tool of the God and the Goddess."

Repeat the same step by passing the broom through the smoke of the incense:

"This broom, this tool of the craft

born from my hands and born from my heart,

I pass it through Air to cleanse, to charge and to bless,

This broom is now a tool of the God and the Goddess."

Now take up your holy water, stand above the broom and sprinkle the broom with holy water whilst repeating:

"This broom, this tool of the craft

born from my hands and born from my heart,

I wash it now with holy water to cleanse, to charge and to bless,

This broom is now a tool of the God and the Goddess."

Take up your broom and with the bristles facing upward repeat the following chant as many times as needed, ending the last time with *"As I will, so mote it be."*

"Divine mother and father, universal spirit above,

Charged this broom is now and devoid of

Any mundane purpose, task or charge,

It is empowered to cleanse, to banish and to recharge,

Any space I choose worthy,

This my magickal broom is now ready!"

"As I will, so mote it be."

Samhain Pumpkin Fritter Critters

Pumpkin fritters go with almost any meal and they're great on their own as well. Here is a fail-safe recipe to use.

What you will need:

- 1 teaspoon Vanilla extract
- 1 beaten egg
- 1 cup of self-raising flour
- 2 full cups of pumpkin (smashed)
- 1 pinch of salt
- 1 tablespoon brown sugar
- Sunflower oil to fry the fritters

Critter coating (optional but great for Samhain)

- 50g refined sugar
- 3 teaspoons Cinnamon

In a big mixing bowl add the smashed pumpkin, Vanilla extract and the egg, mix well. Now add the self-raising flour, pinch of salt, brown sugar and mix again until you get a well-mixed consistency.

Heat the oil in a frying pan on the stove. Add a pinch of the mixture to see when the oil is ready. When it is ready spoon a spoonful of mixture at a time and fry them until they are golden brown on both sides. Scoop them out on a plate and coat the pumpkin fritter critters with the mix of refined sugar and cinnamon mix.

YULE

Yule is celebrated on the longest night of the year and the shortest day. This is the Winter Solstice. It is the birth of the *Child of Promise.* Yule is celebrated with Yule logs, evergreen Fir trees to represent everlasting life. The entire celebration of Yule is customarily started 12 days before the longest night and shortest day. In the Pagan Asatru faith, the 12 days of Yule are an exceptional celebration of feasting and merry making.

Yule is traditionally a Germanic festival that calls in the promise of the New Year. For Witches though, Yule is not the New Year, it is the time when all the old is disposed. It is the moment that the Sun

God is born. To explain this, he is born from the womb which was the tomb. It is a metaphorical birth from the depths of the underworld into the light of the earth. The days will get longer now, and the nights will get shorter, and so, the immortal promise of the continuation of life has been fulfilled and therefore all the old must go.

Yule presents are exchanged, and the presents are usually meant to be things that you no longer use and believe someone else could. These presents are to be left under the community Fir tree. When it is time, each person or family may go to the tree and pick a present. Once the presents have been taken, it is customary to give thanks for the bountiful life that each person has. Gratitude is the attitude of Yule and the process is called Wassail. A token of thanks is given, and the glass / goblet is raised and when the person is done giving thanks to the people, and to the gods, they declare "WASSAIL!"

In a traditional Germanic Yule ritual, the Galdr, or runes are called in to invoke the Father God, Odin. When it is time for the workings there will be a rune pouch handed around by the High Priestess and each person present will take a rune from the pouch. The rune is the forecast and advice for the coming months. There are generally six copies of each rune in the pouch and only the rune Ansuz is singular.

The most prominent symbols of Yule are the Holly and Mistletoe. Their resemblance to the goddess and the god is important to know and represents the presence of fertility within the divine couple even in the coldest and longest night of the year. The red berries from the Holly tree represent the menstrual cycle of the goddess and the ability of her being able to bare children. The Mistletoe berries are found in an array of colours but for Yule the white berries are important because they represent the masculine reproductive fluid of the god.

Yule is also no time to celebrate the god and goddess on the altar. There are two reasons for this. Firstly, the god is a new-born babe, born from the darkness, the womb that was the underworld tomb, and has no understanding of ruling or of being worshipped. You are welcome to place a baby statue on the altar to welcome his return as the growing oak king, however there is no logical explanation for having him on the altar during Yule. The goddess is also not present because she is still traversing the underworld landscape and will not be present at the altar until after Imbolc when we hear her first stirrings under the earth.

Altar Dressings

- Various reds, greens and white cloths and drapes
- Mistletoe
- Holly
- Horns for drinking and Wassail
- A babylike representation of the Oak God
- Imagery of the returning of the sun
- Runes – Elder Futhark work best
- Boar-shaped bread or entire boar on the spit
- A yule log
- Golden candles
- White candles
- Fir tree
- Presents for all present
- Wreaths
- Juniper berries and oils
- Birch wood or Birch oil

Crafts and Arts

Yule Log Cake

What you will need:

- 4 Large Eggs separated
- ¾ Cup Castor Sugar
- 1 teaspoon Vanilla Essence
- ¾ Cup Cake Flour
- 1 teaspoon Baking powder
- ¼ teaspoon salt
- Chocolate Icing

Begin by beating the egg yolks together until thick, then add the vanilla essence into the mix. Mix the flour, baking powder and add to the egg and vanilla mix. Stir until mixed thoroughly. Beat the egg whites and the salt together until they are stiff but not dry.

Using a metal spoon fold the egg whites and salt into the batter. Please be gentle. Line your Swiss roll tin with wax paper and pour the batter into the tin. Bake for 15 – 25 min in a preheated oven at 356°F. Now mix the chocolate icing. (cream works better than milk, but it does make it richer.) Once the yule log is finished baking roll it out onto a damp cloth immediately. Turn it onto castor sugar and peel off the wax paper. Spread the chocolate icing onto the yule log and begin rolling it. Allow it to cool. A secret is to place it in a very cool dark place. If you would like to add extra sprinkles of red and green on top, feel free to do so.

Wassail Yule Mead

What you will need:

- 600ml Honey
- 250ml Strong Rooibos Tea
- 2 Large lemons
- 25g Brewer's Yeast
- 2 teaspoons white sugar
- 1 teaspoon cinnamon
- 1 teaspoon ginger

- 2.5 Litres Water
- Fermentation vessel

Add yeast and sugar together in a bowl and mix. Add warm water to soak the ingredients, cover with cling film and allow to set. In a large pot, bring the 2.5 litres of water to the boil and begin stirring in the honey. Do this at a low heat so that the honey does not burn or harden inside the water. Add the cinnamon and the ginger, continue stirring for 15 minutes. Take it all off the stove and add lemon pieces to the mix. Allow this mixture to stand for at least 45min.

Ensure that the yeast mixture now has a foamy consistency and add it to the honey mix. Add all of this to your fermentation vessel and allow it to ferment for 5 – 6 weeks.

IMBOLC

The Quickening is another name for Imbolc. It is also known as Candlemas, Oimelc, Brigid's Day and Brigantia. Imbolc literally means in the belly or ewe's milk. It is the time when most of the cattle on the farms began producing milk. This was a joyous time for the people because they knew that spring was on her way.

The Child of Promise that was born at Yule now becomes *The Conquering Child.* The story of John Barleycorn also runs through the Wheel of the Year, and he is now brought into the home. The great Celtic goddess of poetry and crafting, healing and childbirth is venerated on this day. In her honour and in the honour of all those gods and goddesses who have had a hand in the Tuatha Dé

Danaan, it is customary to make a Brigid's cross and hang it in your home for protection and peace.

The story of the goddess is far more prevalent at Imbolc. She has finally been able to successfully pass through the darkness of the underworld and she is now stirring beneath the earth. The whole earth begins to change in her presence and that is why Imbolc is such an important festival. It is important to keep her as the maiden on the altar. She is not yet on the earth's surface, but she is home under the sun.

There is a more important part of Imbolc than the tale of the god and goddess. That importance comes from within each one of us. Imbolc is laden with whites and bright greens, with this new light colour change in the homes and on your altar, your inner workings should also begin to change and to single out everything that you wish to plant at Ostara. Imbolc is a time of great preparation and planning.

It is also this preparation and planning that is the reason that most witches choose this time for initiations, dedications to the gods, rededications and new pledges that they may have found with the new turn of the wheel. When following the wheel of the year in your life, you will begin to see that there is indeed a time for everything and by syncing your life in with the great wheel, you will begin to understand your own inner workings much better.

There is a time for peace and quiet, a deep stillness that leads to introspection, some may refer to this as depression, but it is not, it is simply a time when the soul needs that deep stillness and the world needs to allow it. Then there is a time for celebrating life, initiating into the new turn of the wheel, of planting and of reaping what you have sown. All this is what is understood in turning the wheel of the year.

Altar Dressings

- White drapes with light greens
- John Barleycorn from Lammas
- Snowdrops and late winter bulbs
- Maiden goddess statue
- Milk products (Breads, cheese, milk)
- Flowers
- Symbols of the first signs of spring
- Sun Wheels
- Brigid's Cross

CRAFTS AND ARTS

Brigid's Cross

What you will need:

- Approximately eight to fifteen grass reeds
- A scissors
- Some white cotton

The Brigid's Cross gets easier to make the more you practice. If you do not have access to reeds or strong enough blades of grass, then use green raffia, pipe cleaners or anything strong enough.

Even creating the Brigid Cross from green strips of paper works for writing the blessings on the paper and creating the Brigid's Cross. Make use of what you have. It is the intention that counts.

Directions for creating the Brigid cross

1. Lay your first reed straight down in front of you
2. Fold a second reed over the first as shown in the image below

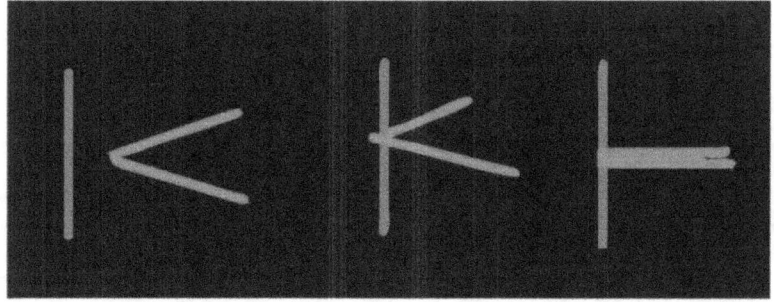

3. Then take a new reed and repeat the process as in the image below

4. Repeat this process until you are happy with the size of your Brigid's cross. Remember to hold the centre of the cross with your thumb to keep everything in place.

5. Now tie the ends together with your white cotton. As you do this repeat the following chant:

    "Brigid, great Goddess of Poetry and Healing,

    Brigid, great Goddess of Smith craft and midwifery,

    Lady of the Tuatha de Danaan, daughter of Dagda,

    I call you to bring peace and prosperity from afar,

    Our home is yours, the Spring is here,

    Goddess Brigid, remove the bane, remove the fear,

    Protect this home and accept my prayer,

    As I ask, so it shall be done,

    The Goddess brings in the strengthening of the sun!"

6. When you are done with the entire process your Brigid's Cross should look like this:

What does a Brigid's Cross symbolise?

The Brigid's Cross is a symbol of protection and peace in the home. It is allowing the Goddess Brigid entrance into your home and petitioning her to keep baneful energies at bay. It is also symbolising the presence of Imbolc and welcoming in the spirit of Spring and the strengthening of the sun, the greening of the fields and the prosperity of the home. To many witches, Imbolc is not Imbolc without the presence of the Brigid's Cross.

OSTARA

Ostara is a time of extreme joy for the people of the earth and for the gods. Not only does Persephone return to her mother, Demeter and to the land of the living, but the very birds are physiologically changed, and egg production is stimulated the second that their retinae are exposed to more than 12 hours of sunlight.

Ostara is the celebration of the fertility of the earth returning, hence the presence of beautifully decorated and multi-coloured eggs. Ostara is also known as the vernal equinox, meaning that the day and night are now equal, and the days will now get longer, and the nights will get shorter. The entire festival is named after the Goddess Eostre, a Germanic Goddess who has almost no record besides the written excerpt below from the Benedictine Monk, Bede:

"Eostur-monath, qui nunc Paschalis mensis interpretatur, quondam a Dea illorum quæ Eostre vocabatur, et cui in illo festa celebrabant nomen habuit: a cujus nomine nunc Paschale tempus cognominant, consueto antiquæ observationis vocabulo gaudia novæ solemnitatis vocantes."

[Giles (1843:179)] Citation enter

In the above excerpt Bede mentions that the people worshipped a Goddess Eostre but now they have what is known as the 'Paschal month' and in this festival they have taken her honoured feasts and celebrations and have attributed it instead to a new rite and a new name.

Sadly, not much is known about this Goddess, however Spring is more than a change in festival names or feasting mannerisms. Spring is about starting new things, planting the seeds to harvest at Lammas and again at Mabon. It is imperative that you plan at Imbolc, and plant at Ostara so that your harvest at Lammas and at Mabon will be bountiful.

Other names for Ostara are: Lady Day, Earrach, Alban Eilir and the Festival of Trees. This festival is about balance and growth.

Altar Dressings

- Seedlings in trays.

- Green, white and light-coloured altar cloths.

- Statues of rabbits or hares.

- Daffodils and other flowers.

- Rose and Violet oil.

- Your decorated Ostara eggs.

- For cakes and ale, make some seed cake.

- Green reeds or bundles of green grass to hang around the ritual area.

- Cowrie shells to represent fertility.

- Butterfly imagery.

CRAFTS AND ARTS

Ostara Poppy Cake

What you will need:

Frosting (Optional)

- Fresh Thyme leaves
- Strips of Lemon zest
- 250g icing sugar
- Edible flowers

For the cake

- 20cm bread baking tin
- 3 Large eggs
- 2 Teaspoons Vanilla extract

- 150g Castor Sugar
- 150g Flour (Self-Raising)
- 2 Large lemons
- 2 Tablespoons Poppy seeds
- 3 Tablespoons fresh Milk

Directions:

- Before you begin, pre-heat your oven to 180 °C.
- Mix the Vanilla, eggs and milk together in a large bowl.
- Mix the dry ingredients (sugar, flour, lemon zest from the two lemons, and poppy seeds) together in a separate bowl.
- Now begin adding the wet ingredients to the dry ingredients. Do this step very slowly to ensure a fluffy cake.
- Beat the mixture very well.
- Butter your bread tin and add in the mixture.
- Bake for 50 – 60 minutes, keeping a careful eye on the oven.
- To decorate your cake, mix the juice from the lemons with the icing sugar. Wait for the cake to cool and then add the icing on top in any fashion that you would like. Sprinkle Thyme and edible flowers to give it that Ostara feel.

BELTANE

Beltane, or May Day is the main fertility rite in the Wheel of the Year. It is the time of the Great Hunt. The moment when the Horned God in his image of the Oak King chases down the Goddess and mates with her. This is also the time when pagans across the world dance the Maypole. The significance of the Maypole is not always understood; however, it is always enjoyed. The Maypole symbolises the phallus of the God being wrapped by the ribbons. These ribbons symbolise the womb and sexual organs of the Goddess. It is this union that brings in the harvest.

Beltane is also one of the prime moments in the Wheel of the Year to get married. To quote Starhawk: "This is the time when sweet desire weds wild delight." If you do not have a partner, but do want to get married, you would make your wish when jumping over the bel-fire. The bel-fire and the maypole are two distinct representations of this festival.

Beltane is also right across from Samhain on the Wheel, and this means a thinning of the veil between man and spirit. Beltane is the most sought-after time for those who believe in the world of faery. It is very disrespectful, even if you don't believe in them, not to make a separate table with milk, whisky and cookies or some of your food for the wee folk. If you keep to this tradition, definitely expect a gift from them in the morning.

Altar Dressings

- Red, pink, white and green altar cloths.
- Mini maypole.
- Hawthorn blossoms.
- Fae imagery.
- Fertility symbols.
- A replica of the lover's statue: The Kiss by Rodin can be used to symbolise the god and goddess.
- Make sure to have the Bel-Fire as well as a broom to jump if anyone does not wish to jump the fire.

CRAFTS AND ARTS

Beltane Fae Cakes

What you will need:

- 100g Self-Raising flour
- 100g Butter
- 2 Large eggs
- 2 Teaspoons Vanilla essence
- 100g Castor sugar

To make the Icing:

- Hundreds and thousands or any other glitter and sprinkle decorations
- 150g Icing Sugar

- Fresh cream

Directions:

- Pre-heat the oven to 175 °C
- Mix the sugar and the butter together, adding in the vanilla essence.
- Slowly add the eggs and carry on beating the mixture.
- Fold the flour into the mixture.
- Butter the muffin tray.
- Spoon one tablespoon of mixture into each muffin spacing.
- Bake for 20 minutes or until golden brown.
- Mix the icing sugar and the cream until you are happy with the consistency.
- Ice the fae cakes to represent Beltane.

LITHA

Litha is the Summer Solstice. This is the longest day in the year, but also the battle between the Oak King and his dark counterpart, the Holly King. The Oak King, the Sun King, loses this battle and is fatally wounded. The metaphor speaks about how the sun will begin to wane from this day onwards.

Litha is also known by other names such as Samradh, Alban Hefin, Aerra Litha, and of course Mother Night. This is the time when the goddess begins to dance the dance of death. She twirls around the wounded King, and he is certain that he is going to have to be consumed by her at Lammas. He accepts his fate and does not deny that victory belongs to the Holly King.

Litha belongs to the fire element, it is also the hottest day in the year according to the mythology. This is the zenith of the sun. It will now give over to the darker half of the year. This is also your last attempt at pushing to harvest what you wish to harvest in this turn of the wheel of the year.

One of the most important themes throughout Litha, is gratitude for life. Gratitude for the oak king giving his life, gratitude for our lives, no matter what they look like. Gratitude should be something that we actively express every day in our life, however many people forget and for this reason, Litha is the celebration of gratitude.

Altar Dressings

- Roses
- Sunflowers
- Oak leaves
- Symbols of the sun
- Red, yellow and green altar cloths
- Holly leaves can be added, but this is the celebration of the life of the Oak King.
- Lavender sprigs
- Chamomile flowers.

- Robed image of the goddess in mourning, or seen as doing the dance of death

CRAFTS AND ARTS

Litha Oak Wreath

What you will need:

- Willow branches
- Oak branches, leaves and acorns
- Red embroidery cotton
- Material sunflowers

Directions:

- Plait the willow branches together to form the basis for your wreath. Tie the ends if need be with the red embroidery cotton.
- Place the Oak branches, leaves and acorns into the centre holes of the Willow.
- Put the material sunflowers into the wreath as well and design it as you wish.
- Use the red cotton to tie any of the decorations.

When you have completed the wreath, hold it to the sky with the sun shining through the middle of it. Repeat this chant until you feel that you have soaked in the strength of the sun long enough to hold out until Yule.

"Oak King's sacrifice, pinnacle of your prowess,

Grant me your light as you heal through the Goddess,

Grant me your strength as the wheel turns to darkness,

Grant me your light so I may reminisce,

Shine for me until you are born again,

Shine for me until you return to the world of men.

Grateful I am for all you have done,

Great Oak God of the Sun."

LAMMAS / LUGHNASADH

The first harvest has finally come. It is time now to reap what you have sown. This is also the sacrifice of the Lord of the Grain known also as John Barleycorn. The great Celtic God Lugh is sacrificed to feed the people of Tuatha Da Danaan. If you have followed the Wheel of the Year as best as you could, then this is your first sight of reaping everything that you have worked so hard at achieving.

The first harvest is also known as the grain harvest or the bread harvest. We also catch sight of Demeter, mother of the grain at this festival. Her story, and the story of Lugh are prominent pieces in the traditional coven practices. One must choose the themes though, as this festival is filled with many themes from many pantheons.

John Barleycorn is sacrificed at Lammas, it is also customary to make little John Barleycorn's to keep as a remembrance and to take out at Imbolc to burn for the new ideas. This John Barleycorn will hold all the effort and the blood, sweat and tears of this turn of the wheel of the year.

John Barleycorn must die

Traffic – Steve Winwood

"There were three men came out of the west, their fortunes for to try
And these three men made a solemn vow
John Barleycorn must die

They've plowed, they've sown, they've harrowed him in
Threw clods upon his head
And these three men made a solemn vow
John Barleycorn was dead

They've let him lie for a very long time, 'til the rains from heaven did fall
And little Sir John sprung up his head and so amazed them all
They've let him stand 'til midsummer's day 'til he looked both pale and wan

And little Sir John's grown a long beard and so become a man

They've hired men with their scythes so sharp to cut him off at the knee
They've rolled him and tied him by the way, serving him most barbarously
They've hired men with their sharp pitchforks who've pricked him to the heart
And the loader he has served him worse than that
For he's bound him to the cart

They've wheeled him around and around a field 'til they came onto a pond
And there they made a solemn oath on poor John Barleycorn
They've hired men with their crabtree sticks to cut him skin from bone
And the miller he has served him worse than that
For he's ground him between two stones

And little Sir John and the nut brown bowl and his brandy in the glass
And little Sir John and the nut brown bowl proved the strongest

man at last

The huntsman he can't hunt the fox nor so loudly to blow his horn

And the tinker he can't mend kettle or pots without a little barleycorn"

ALTAR DRESSINGS

- Corn dollies
- Grains of all kinds
- Breads with seeds
- A large John Barleycorn to sacrifice
- Sickles
- Beige, white, tan coloured altar cloths

CRAFTS AND ARTS

John Barleycorn

What you will need:

- An old man's outfit
- Hay (Lots of it)
- String
- A straw hat
- A strong branch that will hold John Barleycorn

Directions:

- Stuff the outfit with hay, almost like a body, tying the pieces together with the string.
- Leave hay to come out of the shirt so that you can prop the hat on top of it.
- Dig a hole where the fire pit will be.
- Now place the strong branch through the leg of the pants and into the back of the shirt.
- Prop John barleycorn into the newly dug hole.
- Set him alight and whilst he is burning sing the lyrics to the song, John Barleycorn must die above.

MABON

Mabon is the Autumnal Equinox, meaning, once again day and night are equal, but this time, the nights will grow longer, colder, and as they do, we will know that the Oak King is trudging through the lessons of the underworld.

The Goddess is said to devour the god during the night of Mabon. He will enter her tomb and will emerge again at Yule. It is the second harvest and the last time to reap what you have sown. Beyond being the second harvest, Mabon is also the wine harvest and the fruit harvest. It is said that the last of the soul of the god is in the fruit and when we eat them, we must remember how he sacrificed himself, so that we may be fed and survive the long, dark winter months ahead.

ALTAR DRESSINGS

- Apples
- Autumn leaves
- Acorns
- Pinecones
- Antlers
- Vines
- Your knot magick

CRAFTS AND ARTS

Clove Orange House Cleanser

What you will need:

- 1 or more large oranges (the amount depends on how many you wish to make)
- 1 Packet of whole cloves

Directions:

- Even though the 'Clove Orange House Cleanser' is easy to make, it is a powerful cleanser on the mundane and in the spiritual world.
- Pierce the orange with the clove buds.
- You can place as many as you wish.
- Before placing your 'Clove Orange House Cleanser' around your home, hold it in both hands and repeat this chant:

"Orange and clove, together as one,

Fight off negativity from my home."

Now place them around the house. They are great for fighting off mosquitoes and all sorts of insects. On the spiritual they ward off negativity. Make sure to make a new one every week.

The Path of the Masculine through the Wheel of the Year

The Wheel of the Year is really all about tracing the path of the Sun God. It is simultaneously the path of the Oak King, one of the aspects of the Sun God, and the Holly King, another aspect of the Sun God.

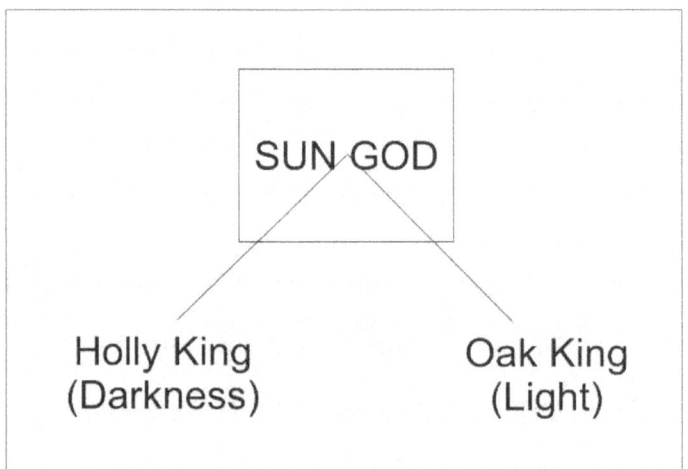

The Wheel of the Year is also a dated according to the movement of the sun, therefore it is a celebration of the solar timing. The sun god has been venerated throughout history, almost every single native culture worshipped the sun and petitioned it throughout the winter months to return. According to the geographical placement of the people who were worshipping, their prayers as well as their attributes given to their version of the sun god would mirror their surroundings.

Within the Wiccan framework created by Gardner, we witness a dualistic viewpoint of the sun god or the solar aspect of the Horned God. The sun god is divided into light and dark. The Oak King governs the light half of the year which begins at Yule with his return from the underworld and ends at Litha when he is fatally wounded in battle by the Holly King. The Holly King then reigns from Litha until Yule when it is his longest night.

The dualistic nature of the sun god is a necessary addition to the already complex story of the Wheel of the Year. We all have a shadow side as well as a light side. We cannot know the heat if we do not understand the cold. We cannot identify happiness if we have not felt sadness. The masculine path is no different throughout this solar wheel, it must contain a dualistic nature so that we humans can understand and give meaning to what is happening around us.

To worship the sun god in his totality, we need to understand every aspect of him. We need to identify and study his darkness and walk the path with him through the end of summer into autumn and through winter. We need to understand his shadow self is within us as well and we need to locate that darkness within us and take control over it. Similarly, the Oak King must also be understood, we must understand his strength through the light and with him we must descend into the darkness and ensure that we do not see the descent as a fall of any kind, it is simply a rising into a different aspect of ourselves.

THE PATH OF THE FEMININE THROUGH THE WHEEL OF THE YEAR

The goddess is always in everything. If you recall, we mentioned earlier how she is the darkness and the void, how she is the potential of everything in the universe. How can there be any fable then without her? She is always found in either the maiden, mother or crone aspect.

Like with the dualistic nature of the god that runs through the Wheel of the Year, the goddess mimics his movements, but can also find herself in various stages at the same time. Her maiden phase only begins at Imbolc, where his light reign begins at his birth from the tomb (resurrection) at Yule. She is then quickly sprung into a teenager by the time Ostara comes but can also appear as Mother Nature, as Ostara / Eostre, or she can become any other goddess that you wish to venerate on that festival.

She descends on Samhain, and for two festivals, Samhain and Yule she remains the old hag, the crone, the wise woman of bone and medicine. However, she is not only darkness in the crone stage, she can bring darkness, like she does on Mabon when the Oak King finally descends back into her womb (which is the underworld and the tomb). In this aspect, and at this moment on the wheel she is the dark mother who sacrifices her husband to feed the people of the earth.

Everything has a cycle, the cycle of the goddess, even though it is not always celebrated or spoken of within the wheel, is as important as the cycle of the god, if not more so. It is she who assists the god at fulfilling his duties and his birth rights at every turn. Whether she is his mother, his maiden lover, his death-defying crone, she is the one who makes his journey possible.

Chapter 3 – Forging your Witch-Self

It is now time that you learn to forge your witch-self. It is now time to step into your own power and to grasp the entirety of what and who you are. For you to know what your strengths and your gifts are, you must be able to step into this power without fear of the unknown. The unknown is the goddess, and how can you fear her? Respect is unquestionably one of the most paramount things when beginning on this path and you should never ever disrespect spirit. Especially if you do not completely understand it yet. Funnily enough, one can never understand spirit completely, it is indeed an enigma to humanity and may remain like that until the end of all things mundane.

To forge your witch-self, there are a few tips, tricks and tools to get you started. Remember the most important part of all of this is to listen to your intuition. If something does not feel right, then please do not even think of doing it. We are all unique and your path will be your own. It must be so.

THE WICCAN REDE

The Wiccan Rede, as it is known now, is one of the handiest references that you can choose to listen to and study when you are beginning on your path. It was first published by a hereditary witch named Lady Gwen Thompson in a magazine called the Green Egg. She claims that it was her grandmother who gifted her this wisdom. Sadly, not everything can be proved, and it is thought that Doreen Valiente, ritual architect to Gerald Gardner, spoke the "an harm it none, do what ye will" words in a public speech before the counsel of the wise ones or the Rede of the Wiccae was even published.

We will never know who wrote it first, or where it came from, but the reason it is such a brilliant reference is because it works. The Wiccan Rede stands true to its wisdom and many, Wiccans and Witches know it well. For your convenience the most important pieces have been set in Bold. These are pieces that should be researched and meditated upon.

The Rede of the Wiccae *(Counsel of the Wise Ones)*

Written and published by Lady Gwen Thompson in the Ostara Edition of the Green Egg Magazine (1975)

Bide the Wiccan Law ye must,

In Perfect Love and Perfect Trust;

Live ye must and let to live,

Fairly take and fairly give.

True in love, ever be,

Lest thy love be false to thee.

With a fool no season spend,

Nor be counted as his friend.

Soft of eye and light of touch,

Speak ye little, listen much.

Ever mind the rule of three,

What ye send out comes back to thee.

This lesson well, thou must learn

Ye only get what ye do earn.

Eight words the Wiccan Rede fulfill -

An it harm none, do as ye will.

***Deosil** go by **waxing** Moon,*

*Sing and dance **the invoking** Rune;*

***Widdershins** go by **waning** Moon,*

*Chant ye then a **freeing** tune;*

*When the Lady's **Moon is new**,*

*Kiss thy hand to Her **times two**;*

*When the **Bow rides in the eve***

*Turn to what you would **achieve**;*

*When the **Moon rides at her peak**,*

*Then thy heart's desire **seek**;*

*When the **Sickle shows Her face***

***Release** the old with proper grace.*

Greet the Days and greet the Nights

With joy and thanks for all delights.

Sing the seasons all around

Til wondrous awe and love abound

Heed the **North wind**'s *mighty gale,*

Lock the door & trim the sail;

*When the **wind comes from the South**,*

***Love** will kiss thee on the mouth;*

*When the **wind blows from the West**,*

*Hearts will find their **peace and rest**;*

*When the **wind blows from the East**,*

*Expect **the new** and set the feast.*

***Nine woods** in the Cauldron go,*

Burn them quick and burn them slow;

***Grape** and **fir** and **apple** tree,*

*And **Hawthorn** are sacred to Thee,*

Willow, hazel, rowan, birch,

*And **oak** will guide your every search;*

Elder be the Lady's tree -

Burn it not or cursed ye'll be.

***Birchwood** in the fire goes*

*To tell us **true what Goddess knows**.*

***Oak** trees tower great with might,*

*Burn the Oak for **God's insight**.*

***Rowan** is a tree of power*

*Causing **life and magic** to flower.*

***Willows** at the waters stand*

*To help us to the **Summerland**.*

Hawthorn burn to purify

And draw the faerie to your eye.

Hazel tree, the wisdom sage,

Lends strength that comes with honored age.

White the flowers of Apple tree,

The holy gift of fecundity.

Grape grows upon the fruitful vine,

Sacred gifts of joy and wine.

Fir's ever greenness declares life

Succeeds beyond any strife.

Heed ye flower, bush, and tree,

And by the Lady Blessed be.

Where the rippling waters flow

Cast a stone and truth ye'll know;

Four times the Major Sabbats mark

In the light and in the dark:

As the old year starts to wane

The new begins with dark Samhain.

When flowers blossom through the snow

Fair Brigid casts her seed to sow.

When winter yields to warmth's return

Let the Beltane fires burn.

As summer turns to Lammas night

First fruits and Grain Gods reach their height.

Four times the Minor Sabbats fall

Use the Sun to mark them all:

At Yuletide, with feast and mirth

We celebrate the God Child's birth.

Spring Equinox, Eostara's fest,

All newborn creatures will be blessed.

When the Sun has reached its height

Celebrate the greatest Light.

Offer thanks at second reaping;

Mabon poised for winter's sleeping.

Cast the **circle thrice about**,

To keep unwelcome **spirits out**.

To **bind** the **spell** well every time,

Let the spell be **spake in rhyme**.

Follow this with mind & art,

Bright the cheeks and warm the heart,

And merry meet & merry part

And merry meet again!

FINDING YOUR WITCH NAME

Ah, the task of being given a name. A name of the craft that would provide you with the persona of the Witch within. The name that you choose is extremely important. Many enjoy names that contain their totem animals and their favourite time of day and that is perfectly alright if you like that. The name though, the one that you use in your craft and in front of your deities should never ever be known by anyone but you and the gods. Why? Because your name will become like your blood and your hair, dangerous in the wrong hands.

The craft name is the name you take up and the persona (which should be a completely open self) in front of the gods and your spirit allies. This is your work, your name, your path. There is nothing in that sentence that really has anything to do with anyone else. Many authors have witchy names for the public and then they have their private ones for their own path. It is this personal private magically exclusive to your own path name that you will be guided to find here. You wouldn't allow the person down the road the keys to your home and allow them to go through your things, would you? Then why give the whole world access to you on the astral and on the physical. Yes, this name is that important. It is you. So be wise and keep this name hidden, known only to you and to the spiritual realm. Do not even mention it to your High Priestess or elders, for everyone walks a path together for a season and not everyone is as nice as you would like them to be. Rather be safe than sorry.

Why do you need a Witch name in the first place? Your Witch name allows your subconscious to begin creating the persona that you have with spirit. It begins allowing you to store the spiritual experiences away from the mundane. When you have been practicing for a long while, you will find that you can hop in and out of your meditation or trance state and this is imperative if you are going to be assisting people who live solely in the mundane world. Your witch name is also important because you are able to shield your spiritual work on the astral. You are protected by using a spiritual name and shielded from jealous attacks on your spiritual self.

Some argue that having more than one name will cause a rift in the mind, a sort of split personality. We are not such vulnerable creatures. Yes, mental instability and mental problems do exist, and sometimes they are an intense hindrance to our lives. However, the soul knows best. If your mental state is prone to mental disorders and choosing another name does not feel right, then by all means, do not have another one. Many witches that I have met only use a name in public circle because they have too. A great many other witches whom I call friend, only found their names years after starting out on the path. So, whatever feels comfortable and right, you do that, because that is you, and you are perfect exactly the way that you are.

CHOOSING YOUR NAME THROUGH DREAMWORK

If dreaming is your thing, then you are very fortunate indeed. The dreamscape is the direct channel of information to and from the subconscious mind. There are so many avenues to investigate through the dreamworld that witches find dreaming one of the most important skills to have. Connecting with your Witch name through dreamwork is easier than you may think. There are many ways to accomplish this, and if you are a lucid dreamer then the path is easier. For this book though, we will be advising name finding through normal dream states.

UTILISING THE PLANT KINGDOM FOR DREAMWORK

The plant kingdom can be extremely helpful, and if you have an interest in plants, trees and flowers then hedge witchery may be your thing. There are thousands of plants that can assist us in entering an altered state in our dreams and help us to manage our dream recall better. It is more often than not that many of these plants are poisonous to the system and for that simple reason, without the proper medical background it would be unwise to go down that path. There are however other plants that work quite as well, and they provide us with lifelong allies into the dreamscape.

Lavendula Officianalis

Lavender is not a sissy plant as many like to call it. In fact, Lavender may be one of the most beloved plants known to witches. Using Lavender to enter the dreamscape is definitely a safe enough doorway and will not produce any side effects from a single dose. Lavender does however produce a heightened release of female hormones into the body and so it is not advisable for men / boys to be using this plant over a long period of time. Make yourself a cup of Lavender Tea, keep a sprig of Lavender aside. Using a perfectly square piece of blue paper, write your name as it is now. Then write and speak the following words:

"Lavender light I honour and petition you,

My witches name revealed to me,

In dreamscape give me eyes to see,

As I will so mote it be!"

When you are done, fold the sprig of Lavender into the blue square of paper. Place it under your pillow. Drink your Lavender tea and keep a journal next to your bed with a pen. Repeat this entire process until your Witch name appears to you. It will come. Believe and you will receive.

Valerian Officianalis

The Valerian spirit is strong. It is also one of the most foul-smelling plants that can be found. It is said that Valerian smells something akin to old wet socks. The Valerian spirit should never be taken without a medical practitioner giving you the go ahead. There are contraindications, there are side effects and you need to be aware of these. Valerian is also a known mutagen and must never be taken during pregnancy.

A powdered version of Valerian is noted by Scott Cunningham as being an excellent substitute for graveyard dust. For the purpose of finding your Witch name, the spirit of Valerian will not only guide, and protect you through the dreamscape but she will also remain an excellent guide for dreamwork after you have acquired your name.

Before doing anything with the Valerian, take approximately half a cup of Valerian root to use over the period of one week. Do this in the waxing lunar phase. Place both your hands over the Valerian and speak the following chant:

> "Mother of the underworld, wise and ancient,
>
> I honour thee.
>
> Mother of the slumber that never returns,
>
> I honour thee,
>
> Valerian, beautiful majestic queen of the night visions,
>
> I honour thee.
>
> I petition thee, to guide and protect me,
>
> I honour thee.
>
> I seek my Witch name from the land of night,
>
> Guide me on my journeys, guide me though the nightscape.
>
> I honour thee."

Try to speak this chant over and over again. Allow it to take you into a trance state by the words and the presence of the Valerian spirit alone. She is with you. She is beneath your hands and you will feel her. Her spirit is strong.

When you are ready make a pot of Valerian tea, add honey to taste. She is not the best tasting medicine, but she is one of the most effective. Make the tea with 1 teaspoon of Valerian per night.

Have a pen and dream journal next to your bed. Please be warned that your dreams will change. If you are not a dreamer and you have chosen to do this to enhance your dreamwork abilities, believe me they will be enhanced. If you encounter any side effects at all, please stop using the Valerian at once.

USING NUMEROLOGY TO FIND YOUR WITCH

NAME

Numerology is the study of numbers. Just like with colour and sound, and pretty much everything else in the universe, numbers also have a vibration. Each number has a universal number attached to it and each letter has a corresponding number. It is believed that numerology predates the Kabbalistic system, but its origins are cloudy. Many people refer back to the work of Pythagoras 569 – 470 BCE, who was a Greek mathematician and great philosopher. His work lends a large amount of information to the face of numerology today. Below is the Pythagorean table used for entrance Numerology.

1	2	3	4	5	6	7	8	9
A	B	C	D	E	F	G	H	I
J	K	L	M	N	O	P	Q	R
S	T	U	V	W	X	Y	Z	

It is this numerology chart that you will be using to see if your name is the right choice for your personality and for what you want to achieve on your path as a Witch. Now we will go into what each of the numbers symbolise. There are thousands of books that go in depth on Numerology, and one such book, which, if you can get your hands on a copy will be one of the most valuable books in your collection is, Cheiro's Book of Numbers. For the sake of simply finding your Witch name, we will only be covering the very basics of Numerology.

The meanings behind the numbers

- The number 1 is the beginning of everything, this is the source number. Number one is the initiator of any project, that first energy burst. Leadership and strength of character are associated with number 1. Number one is akin to the passion, willpower and driving force contained within the element of fire. Beware though, as number 1 is also full of aggression, egotism and contains impulsiveness. Make sure to balance your number 1.

- The number 2 is the number of the empath. It is the number of duality and the dual nature of the universe. Number 2 is the number of mediators and partnerships, healing another and being able to climb into another's shoes. Beware though as the number 2 is also filled with self-consciousness if it is not balanced.

- The number three is the life-giving number. It is the first instance where the dual nature of spirit now gives life. This number is the number of creating more of oneself. It is filled with imagination and great insight. It is known as the number of the artist. There is a downside, and this is the lack of direction, so balancing this number with a more stable input is very necessary.

4

- The number 4 is the filing cabinet of all the other numbers. Number 4 is organisation par excellence. Even though it is said that number 4 is also the practical number it is backed by an attention to detail and a scientific inquiring mind second to none. The caution here, especially when choosing a spiritual Witch name is that number 4 lacks imagination, so pairing it with number 3 or with another imaginative balance is important.

5

- Number 5 is the visionary, the pioneer, the conqueror. Number 5 jumps when needed but sometimes also without looking before they leap. The number 5 loves to explore and delve into a thousand projects and knows them all. The only downside of the number 5 is that they are easily bored and will not study a certain subject in detail. This is unfortunately not helpful in the world of Witchcraft as every single subject must be studied in detail if you are to ever become a teacher in that art or to use it to assist others and yourself. It is no use being a jack of all trades.

6

- The number 6 is the humanitarian of numerology. Sixes are the home bound lovers of life. They are the ones who you can always go to, to borrow a cup of sugar. They are found in the nursing and healing fields and even though they think they know everything; it is seldom found that they don't. The weakness of the 6 is that they will do anything for a person who flatters their efforts, and this is a wide-open doorway for those that wish to use a Witch for all he/she has.

- The number 7 is the seeker of numerology. This number has the ability to delve into the deepest darkest chasms of the void of the Goddess and find the source of all life. Unfortunately, the 7 is a loner, but that is always a trait that many Witches carry. To pick a Witch name vibrating this number means that your intuition and natural occult interests will be at the forefront always. It is more often than not that people with a name carrying the 7 will begin their own religions, mystical paths and they work.

- The number 8 is the name for those wanting to forge ahead to becoming a High Priestess of a coven. The 8's are excellent leaders and they are probably the best at rounding up members to work towards a unified cause. Unfortunately, even though the 8's make brilliant leaders they tend to work far too hard. They are also not in touch with their intuitive side and cannot see the forest for the trees.

9

- The number 9 is the vibration of the writer and the artist. A vibration of neediness does flow through this number however the number is also synonymous with giving back the same or more energy as what is received. Number 9's are extremely selfless and there only real drawback is that they have thousands of interests at once.

Above and beyond the nine main numbers that all things fit into, we have what is known as master numbers. Master numbers have their own special meanings and, in this day, and in this new age, they have also become what is known as angel numbers. We will not be discussing the new age angelic influence, but we will be discussing their original meanings.

The two Master numbers are as follows:

11 – The master number 11 is the spiritual strength of the number 2 amplified a thousand-fold. The negative traits of number two count in number 11 but again, they are amplified.

22 – The master number of 22 is the number of great world changers. 22 is capable of changing the world as we know it. It is also wonderful to see the feats of a 22 within the occult world. Where the negativities apply please see number 4.

Now to the interesting practical magic of choosing your Witch name through Numerology. It is now time for you to go and do some hunting. Find names that you like the meanings of, then work out their numbers like the example below. Try to decide on a number that you want your name to fit into first, then go hunting for the names. These can be the names of animals, birds, colours, gods, goddesses etc.

The Numerology Equation

Using the pythagorean numerology chart above

MORGAINE FOXMOON

4 + 6 + 9 + 7 + 1 + 9 + 5 + 5 + 6 + 6 + 6 + 4 + 6 + 6 + 5 = 85

8 + 5 =

1 + 3 = 4

Number 4 is the number for this name. Now use your birth name to practice and see what attributes your number allows for your personality. Make sure that your Witch name, when you have found it, matches the attributes with which you want to walk your spiritual path.

UTILISING THE METHOD OF BAG DRAWING

There is nothing quite as magical as drawing something out of a bag and finding that it matches you perfectly. If dreaming has not worked, and you wish for something a little faster then why not get a large pouch, even a normal bag will do. Cut out letters, pictures of favourite things and numbers. Make sure that they all fit on the same size papers. Fold them all up. Place them in the bag and say this chant before beginning the picking:

"Bag of chance, pouch of universal synchronicity,

My hand be drawn to the name that is right for me,

Let me pick perfectly what I must,

I know I will, for in the gods I trust."

When you are done, lay the bag in front of you, close your eyes and pick out as many pieces of paper that you feel you need. Less is more in this instance. Once you have your chosen pieces. Open them and sort the options that you have, for example:

The names that come to mind can be as follows:

AWEN CRESCENT BEAR

BEAR OF THE FIRE ECLIPSE

AWEN BEARMOON

Or anything that you feel. You can then use the names that you have jotted down in your journal and work out their numerological attributes and see if it fits with what you would like for your path through the witchcraft landscape. The chances are that it will work the first time that you try. This pouch of chance really does work for almost anything, including divination.

How to Find Your Patron God and Goddess

The first and most troubling question that we hear from neophytes is: "How will I know that they (the gods) are talking to me?" It's all about the faith, the belief and the synchronicity of the moment that it takes place in. Your intuition is always your most powerful tool in understanding the language of the gods.

Devotion is one of the most important parts of Wicca and Witchcraft. Do you need a patron god and goddess? No, you do not need to work with any gods or goddesses. Some hedge witches work with plant allies and have no patron gods or goddesses present. In coven work and through your degrees it is required that you work with at least one god and one goddess, however as a solitary, if this does not suit you then I do not see a problem.

There is so much to learn from the gods and goddesses though. The divine landscape has so many treasure troves to explore and so many beautiful magical gifts to bestow on those who dare to enter into the endless worlds, that it would be a shame not to attempt to work with at least one goddess or one god in your lifetime.

The gods do not only come to you. This is a misconception and a fable that has wormed its way into Witchcraft, and it leaves thousands of witchlings lost and heartbroken because the gods seem to never choose them, yet everyone else has a magical story of how they were chosen. This can cause a horrific rift in the magical growth of the young practitioner and it will affect their practice without them even realising it.

The truth is that the gods have chosen us all. Each and every single person on this earth and in this time has been chosen. You are alive are you not? This is no accident, nor is the fact that you are reading this book and have landed your beautiful eyes on these words. The gods have chosen you. Now, which aspect will you connect with? That is up to you. What do you want to learn, which aspect of the gods do you want as a teacher? Who keeps cropping up in blogs and books? What image do you have in your mind of a god or goddess? Now follow the breadcrumbs, follow them until you find the aspect of the divine that suits you in the moment that you need it.

The aspects of the god and goddess, (remember the diamond theory discussed in Chapter One), do not remain the same, just like you do not remain the same at all. You change. Scientifically, every seven years, you are a physically different person, completely. It is very normal to chop and change aspects of the gods as you, yourself change. It is also extremely normal to have only a single god and goddess your entire life. It depends on you and what feels right for your life.

If this method of seeking out the divine aspects does not suit you then here is a pathworking, a meditation that you can ask someone to read for you, or record it and then make sure you will be undisturbed and that you have your Book of Mirrors or a journal next to you and play the pathworking back to yourself. Using soft repetitive music like the sound of rain on a loop can be extremely helpful as well.

Lie down or sit comfortably. Close your eyes and take a deep breath in through your nose and blow it out your mouth as hard as you can. Breath in again, this time hold the breath for 3 seconds, blow out as hard as you can through your mouth. Again, breathe in and hold for 6 counts... 1...

2... 3... 4... 5... 6... *now breathe out all the worries, the pain, the stress. Breathe in through your nose again and breathe this air into your belly. Breathe out calmly. Place your tongue on the roof of your mouth, right behind your front teeth and get comfortable.*

I want you to place your focus on your feet. Feel your feet relaxing, relax each toe. Now concentrate on your calves, relax them, your thighs, feel how relaxed they are. Your groin area is relaxed, your stomach, your rib cage, relax and allow them gently to feel as though you are drifting off to sleep. Now your chest, relax your chest, your shoulders, your upper arms, your forearms, your hands... relax each finger. Now breathe in and bring your concentration to your neck, allow all the tension to leave your neck, relax. Now your jawbone, relax your cheek muscles your mouth, your eyes and your forehead. Imagine now that you are lying on quicksand, feel your relaxed body sink through the quicksand and land on a concrete slab in a candle lit room.

In this room there are no doors and no windows unless you want them. Imagine now a door in front of you. You have created this door. Look at the markings on the door. Look if there are words or symbols, inspect the door closely. Now, open the door. Behind the door is a white room, again with no doors or windows, unless you want them to be there. Beneath your feet there is a blue cushion. This cushion is positioned right between the white room of light and the concrete room of darkness. Sit down on this cushion. Get comfortable. Now breathe in, and out.

Concentrate now on the doorframe between the two rooms. There is a distinct line between the two and there is a word written on either side. Read them and feel these words in your soul. As you do so a figure appears in one of the rooms. Look toward this figure and greet them. Look at them intently and remember every detail of their face, their hair, their clothing and if they are carrying anything. Is there a change to the room that they have entered? Ask them their name. Ask them why they have come when you called the word written on the doorframe? Ask them for guidance on your path. Ask them how you should practice devotion to them.

When you are ready stand up to greet them. Take the gift that they are handing to you. If another being appears that is okay. Greet them as well. Ask any questions that you may have for them.

When you are ready, walk into the room where the last entity appeared. Stretch your hand upward and as you pull your hand down again, see the ladder from the quicksand above slowly come down so that you can climb back to your mundane self. Climb the ladder upward to your body. Breathe in and release your tongue from the roof of your mouth. Concentrate on your toes. Concentrate on any smells in the air, any sounds, and when you are ready open your eyes and write everything down that you can remember.

This pathworking above assists with meeting any entity that you need to. It is not only used for patron gods and goddesses but remember the three laws of magic are Intention, Focus and

Willpower. So, whatever your intention, focus and willpower is when entering into this meditation, that will be the outcome of the pathworking.

Once you have all the information from the pathworking, make sure to also record your dreams for the next week for more clues on the nature of the being/s in your journey. Pathworking's assist with so many things. They are fantastic for healing, for working out solutions that you cannot otherwise access, they are bridges between the conscious and subconscious minds and pathworking's are a Witch's greatest tool.

THE ALTAR

The Altar is the portal between this side of the veil and the other. It is not only a mundane place where we hope to meet the gods and to pay our respects. The altar is a place on the astral as well. Every time you make an altar, it is opened up on the astral and the sighting of this on the astral of temples, holy places and altars of practitioners that are not shielded on the astral are probably one of the most beautiful memorable sightings that any astral traveller can have.

The altar is also your soul space. Yes, your body may be doing the standing, the kneeling, the seating, but it is your soul that does the devotional motions. This altar is also a place where you show the aspect of the divine that you have chosen to connect to that they are important to you and to your space, that they are allowed into your life.

A witch's altar is sometimes very different to the altar of a Wiccan practitioner. The reason for this is the rules and the adage of *everything has its place within Wicca*. An altar of a non-Wiccan is an arrangement of important symbols and goodies to represent what the witch deems holy and important. The altar can also contain poppets or corn dollies of healing or cursing that the witch may have decided to lay in front of his/her gods. A Witchcraft altar has no segregation for the items, anything goes where he/she pleases. It is however also her place to commune with his/her gods and the altar of a Witch or a Wiccan should never be touched.

The altar of a Wiccan is different in that it has certain placements for each item, even the candles and the incense. A Wiccan altar is divided into three. The back section and the highest level (if your altar has a different level, you can raise the back of the altar by placing a book beneath the cloth) is kept exclusively to represent the Universal spirit. The Universal spirit is only symbolised by a single white candle. Never place a black candle there, whether it is Samhain or not.

Directly in front of the Universal Spirit is the rest of the altar. This place is then divided into left and right. Left and right matched by your left and right when you face your altar. The left is kept exclusively for the goddess and for all things feminine. The right is kept exclusively for the god and for all things masculine. Cakes and ale are never placed on the main altar and a separate table may be placed below this altar. On the left you will set down the feminine elements, the earth and the water. On the right you will place down the masculine elements and those are Air and Fire. Directly in front of the Universal Spirit candle you will have a candle for the goddess on the left and a candle for the god on the right. These two candles do not count as elemental representations.

A statue of your god and goddess can then be added but it is not necessary. Please see the Wiccan altar setup outlined below:

The elements are represented in different ways. For example, you may not have incense on hand, but you have a feather, this is a great representation of Air. It is important to not worry too much on the fine details and to remember that the gods know your intention and your spirit. One of the most important pieces to the working of the altar is the pentacle. The pentacle is a pentagram surrounded by a circle. The pentacle is usually crafted from a natural element and represents the element of Earth. When the pentacle is facing you, your altar is open on the mundane and on the astral and it is an open portal or doorway. When you are finished with your sacred time, you must turn the pentacle over and state that the doorway is closed.

The Wiccan way is to balance everything, the left to the right, the up to the down and the inner to the outer worlds. It is important to balance everything and even though this balance is thought to only be a Wiccan thing, it is not. Mother Nature always seems to balance herself out, we always seem to need balance in our lives, even with food or vitamins that our body craves, we just know it. You know that feeling when you wake up and you really want some orange juice, you can almost taste it, well that is the balance of your body being achieved. Our mind, not our brain, is far more intelligent than we can even begin to comprehend.

Remember this intelligence when you are creating your altar. Remember that this is your souls special place, it belongs to no one but you, or your partner if you both share a sacred space.

SACRED TIME AND SACRED SPACE

You need sacred time and you need your own sacred space. Does this mean that all witches have an entire ritual room to themselves and that they have always had that if they do? Not at all. Sacred time and sacred space have nothing to do with the placement of the devotional practice. Sacred time can be any time you want it to be, sacred space can be anywhere you want it to be. If you do not have the luxury of being brought up by pagan or spiritually alternative parents, then take a walk to the park or go and sit by a tree in the garden. You will find that one day when you do have your own spiritual room or temple space indoors that you long for the time when you sat by the tree.

It does not matter where or when, what matters is that you make the time and you make the space. Cleansing space does not need anything, although sage smudging helps, holy water cleansing does feel a little better but that is only because human beings need to see things happen with their physical eyes. The fact that you go sit by the tree in a park or in your garden or even on the grass in the same spot and intentionally focus your mind and will the place to be cleansed of negativity means that it will be so. That is how powerful your own inner magick is. You need to practice this, and those who do not have the tools at first may seem less fortunate to the untrained practitioner, but in a large sense their training will be far greater.

Your magic is not dependent on the tools that you possess, nor is it dependent on the clothes you wear or the place where you are. You are your magick, your magick lies in the very fibre of your being.

A mental chant for those without a dedicated sacred space

Here is a little chant to remember if you do not have a dedicated sacred space and wish to cleanse, purify and bless the area you are about to sit or stand in:

"I am magick, magick is me,

This ground is holy by my spirit's decree,

I am magick and magick is me,

This ground is sacred, blessed and cleansed

As I will so mote it be!"

A cleansing for those with a dedicated sacred space

If you are fortunate enough to possess a sacred space of your own, then this is a good way to cleanse the space of any baneful or unwanted energetic residue.

First cleanse the space with your besom / broom. If you do not own one, please see the Chapter on Samhain on how to make yourself one. Whilst you are sweeping the energy chant the following words:

> *"Cleanse and cleanse and clean you'll be,*
>
> *Only stay if you're good for me,*
>
> *Cleansing clean energy,*
>
> *The only energy this space will see."*

Now take your holy water, the combined mix of blessed sea salt and preferably blessed mineral water and with your smudge wand or a bunch of feathers, wash the area by sprinkling the holy water over the area and repeating the chant:

> *"Holy, holier, holiest energy be,*
>
> *Washed and blessed, cleansed and dressed,*
>
> *To house the divine and holiest of energy.*
>
> *As I will, so mote it be."*

Now walk the room with your sage incense or smudge stick and allow the air to soak up the scent of sage. Repeat these words as you move about your sacred space:

> *"Sage, my spirit ally I honour you,*
>
> *Vibrate the energy here to house my divinity,*

Sage, my spirit ally, cleanse, bless and make anew,

As I will, so mote it be!"

Now you are ready to cast circle, have devotional practice or simply sit in the divine energetic vibration that you have created. Ensure that you create this space, regardless where in the world you find yourself and under which circumstances. Sacred Time and Sacred Space is far more important than these words can convey. You are building your soul; you are feeding your spirit and you are paving the way to commune with the divine within you and without you. It is only through practicing this sacred time in your intended sacred space that you can ever hope to develop the divine aspects of yourself.

PRACTICING MAGICK VERSUS DEVOTION TIME

Every practitioner wishes to enter the occult because they know they can cause change. It is the sense of power that draws most practitioners to the craft, however the power is already within you. When you say this to a neophyte they usually frown and think you are silly, or you are hiding the path of the real power because you believe that they are not ready yet. The power seekers never stay on the Wiccan path, they meander into other forms of Witchcraft and end up further and further down the rabbit hole. This is their lesson and that is where they find themselves, in the pit of the darkest void of the bosom of the primordial breath of the goddess.

Those who come knocking on the door of the craft because they know that there is more to the origins of their own beings are the ones who are able to remain in Wicca or find themselves a comfortable seat at the table of Witches. Neither the one who seeks power, nor the one who comes for worship and truth are wrong. Everyone has their purpose and their place on this planet and every Wiccan who remains a Wiccan, was always meant to become a Wiccan. Similarly, the Witches who seek to cause harm, have their place. They become the catalysts for other witches to strengthen their protection abilities.

You are divine but you are not a god. You are a spiritual being in a meat suit who is travelling the universe on a giant rock filled with water and sand and life-giving trees around a catastrophically hot ball of fire that gives you your Wheel of the Year. You are living a human life in this moment and therefore the power that you seek will not take you to the place that your soul is searching to be. Devotion to the gods is the necessary bridge that must be built in order for you to:

- Understand your own divine nature
- Identify the divinity within the world around you

- Identify the placement of all circumstances and how they can be changed

- Know what your life purpose is and honour that path

- Find solace in the nature of the evolving world

- Forge a relationship with and learn new gifts from the divine aspects of the dualistic nature of the divine

- Assist the spirits who are trapped on this plain

- Assist the humans who have lost touch with their souls

Devotion is magick without making you a god. Magick requires you to enforce the intended change by utilising the permission from the divine or by yourself. This is impossible if you have not built the bridge to the divine. In Wicca, most covens do not allow a practitioner to practice any form of magick for their entire first degree. This first degree is meant to last only a year and a day but, in many cases, if the practitioner is not ready, they will not be graded.

Begin with creating your sacred space and allotting sacred time to your daily activities. It is the best place to start to know yourself and the divine nature better. The magick is within you, it is not going away, it is with you, it has always been and will always remain there.

The Tools of the Craft

The most important tool of the craft is you. You are your craft, but you will only understand that once you have owned all the tools that there are to own. Like training wheels on a bicycle, the tools of the craft are a necessary teacher for the student to recognise their own potential of practicing magick and of altering their own worlds. We will now cover the most important tools in the craft.

The Besom

The besom is the best cleaning tool of all the options that Witches have to cleanse a space. It can seem like an ordinary grass broom, but to the Witch, this besom can remove all baneful energy from a place, and it does. Many Witches and Wiccans know of sage, they know of holy water, but they do not know of the powerful ally that the besom makes. Not only is the besom a powerful cleanser of the negativity but it is also a bridge between worlds. When the besom is laid down on the ground it becomes a doorway. This doorway is then used in rituals such as handfasting or at Beltane celebrations.

The Wand

The Wand and the Athame have the same duties. They draw and extend the power of the practitioner; they target and focus that energy to a precise pinpointed location. The wand is used, according to Gerald Gardner himself to call nature spirits and those spirits who are threatened by the sight of the Athame. The Wand is masculine in nature, but this will also depend on the tree from which the wand was harvested. The Willow for example is a feminine tree and will cause the wand to display the feminine attributes of the Willow tree as well as the masculine aspects of it being a wand.

The Athame

The Athame is masculine. It is a black handled knife with a double-edged blade used, like the wand, to extend and draw power to and from the practitioner into a focused area such as the perimeter of the circle. It is also never ever to be used to cut anything except ethereal cords and doorways in the circle. The Athame is an astral tool and should be kept as an astral tool.

The Chalice

The Chalice is used as one of the representations of the womb of the goddess. The Chalice is kept on the altar and used in ritual for ale and libation, for the great rite or the condensed form practiced in Gardnerian rituals. The Chalice represents the element of Water on the altar.

The Censor

If you are fortunate enough to own a censor such as the ones seen in the Catholic Church, then that is wonderful. They are excellent tools for space cleansing and preparing by Air. A censor is a closed incense dispenser that hangs on a chain and can be swung to and fro by the practitioner. The censor can be replaced and is more often replaced by an incense holder. It governs the element of Air which is masculine.

The Pentacle

The pentacle, as mentioned in the previous chapter on The Altar, is a representation of the element of Earth and it is a representation of the goddess. The reason that the pentacle is crafted from a natural element such as wood, is because it lends further strength to the fact that it is a tool of the goddess. In Wiccan altars the pentacle is positioned in the centre of the altar because as detailed in previous chapters, the goddess is the origin of all conscious life. Wicca sees the goddess as the origin of all life and therefore the pentacle is the key to opening and closing the altar.

The Cords

Every coven has cords of dedication and initiation. The cords are plaited cloth or rope in varying colours to denote placement and hierarchy. If you are a solitary practitioner, you may create your own initiation cord and use it when you are doing ritual. Originally, they were called cingulum which meant 'belt'. If the practitioner were to leave the coven, the cord would be cut. This would sever both the physical cord and the etheric cords that the practitioner had to the coven and its members. Every coven is different, and colours can vary greatly.

The Robe

Like the magical name, the robe is another trigger into the divine witchcraft nature of the practitioner. The robe allows the mundane to be forgotten and when worn, allows the practitioner to stand fast in their magical personas. The robe is not essential but a helpful tool for all practitioners whether neophytes or experienced. In Wiccan ritual the robe is an essential part of the group mind. Most Alexandrian Wiccans do not use the robe and are seen to be skyclad instead, viewing the nude body as a temple of the gods.

The Boline

The Boline is the white handled sickle shaped cutting blade. The boline is used for all types of mundane cutting. Examples of cutting things on the mundane would be string in a magickal working, herbs for the cauldron, sheets of paper or anything else. The boline is not used for cutting anything on the astral or on the ethereal plains.

The Cauldron

The cauldron is the womb of the goddess. The cauldron contains Awen, it contains the void of potential. It is the most significant representation of the goddess in any ritual. There is no item more likened to the aspects of the feminine divine than the cauldron. The cauldron is used to mix and charge our spells, it is used to burn and banish, welcome in and bless. The cauldron is the eternal goddess, we take our magick, place it in her womb to manifest and we await the birth of our will and her will to be done.

Chapter 4 – Grimoire of Correspondences

The Witch's world is filled with understanding the vibrations and the spirit inherent in each thing, place and creature. A witch makes it their goal to understand these energies to be able to use them in manipulating or altering energy as they see fit. It is this knowledge that the world found to be dangerous, for in the wrong hands, this knowledge can be disastrous.

Even with the understanding and the knowledge of these vibrational signatures, the witch is not a god. You must still answer to the greater powers and you must still ensure that there is always a balance or nature herself will ensure that for you. The natural order of things is no fable and it always bounces back to its original state if the witch is unable or unwilling to follow through with the magick embarked on in the first place.

Correspondences are simply an account of thousands of other accounts of witches and practitioners of the occult. These are the records of years of similar findings of how certain things react and how they behave when used for certain purposes. For example, the knowledge that Orris Root is used extensively in magick to attract permanent romantic love into one's life is not just a fable. This knowledge has been recorded by thousands of practitioners over many years and when the findings are similar, they are kept, being a truth within the landscape of Witchcraft and the occult. It must be noted though, that if you are drawing love into your life, for example, ensure that you have an open space for something new to enter. Declutter, cleanse and make space for the new magick to enter your life and never ever do it when it will cause harm to another being.

Gods, Goddesses and Spirits to Work with in the Beginning

There are thousands of pantheons to choose from. In these pantheons and branches, there are spirits, gods, goddesses and allies from across the veil. There are many who will seek to assist a practitioner in their magickal pursuits without asking for anything more than simple respect and momentary devotion, but there are also those who wish to have a hefty payment in return for their assistance. Before you choose to invoke or evoke a deity or any entity, make doubly sure that you know their history and their lore, their methods of working and records of interaction with practitioners before you even attempt to invite them into your life.

Witchcraft is not child's play; it is not about thinking a salt circle can protect you from being irresponsible. You must practice responsibly and that means understanding who and what you are interacting with and willing to accept the consequences to yourself and to those around you, and that includes the spirits that you choose to interact with.

Another important adage to the Gods, Goddesses and Spirits to work with is the common question on spirit guides and who and what they are. Our spirit guides are generally accepted as those spirits who have passed on and who have made a spiritual soul pact to come back and assist those on earth from the astral. A spirit guide may or may not choose to show themselves to you. Some may communicate through hunches, or feelings, some may communicate through noises and sounds, others may communicate in your dreams or in visions and through meditation. It is also very common to have a *silent* guide whom you never even knew was there.

Guides are not malicious and will never cause you or your family any harm. A spirit or entity that causes harm is something completely different and that is a whole different subject. A guide is a spiritual entity whose compassion and sense of betterment for humanity has driven their soul back into service of those who are still incarnated here on this plane. There are also different spirit guides:

Animal Guides

Animal Guides are extremely common, and almost every person who is in contact with their spiritual side will know what their animal totem is. You can also have more than one animal guide throughout your life. Some animal guides may come to you once and never again. Animals have extremely valuable lessons to teach us and even the sighting of a bee in the morning when you are frantically running around is a sign from the animal kingdom to slow down a little and remember to connect to your inner peace.

Temporary Archetypal Guides

These are guides that show up in a different form to who they are. It may be the form of a Celtic warrior with blue paint running down their face that shows up in a pathworking or meditation. It may be an old woman with far too many wrinkles on her face to be human. They show up in certain forms that will resonate with a part of your soul and nudge you onto the right path or assist you in a time when you need them the most. These guides will never show their true form, unless it is one of your life guides that you have not listened to, who have now sought different ways to reach you. Mostly they go from person to person and only remain where they are needed.

Ancestral Guides

It is not uncommon to have a loved one come back to guide you. This is referred to as a soul pact, and even though the person has passed on, perhaps even before you were old enough to understand how much they loved and cared for you, they will come back to guide you from the astral. Ancestral guides are found in dreams, visions, meditations, pathworking's and even when you're standing in the kitchen alone.

Spirit Guides, Ascended Masters and the Angels

Spirit guides come in all shapes and forms. Many people attest to having angels by their side, or Jesus, Krishna or some of the other ascended masters. Spirit Guides of this nature are usually found with people who counsel many people at any given time. Reiki Masters, Healers, Lightworkers, Charity Doers and Spiritual Teachers usually have an ascended master or well-known spiritual guide at their side. However, it is not only those in the spiritual healing arts who can have the ascended masters. You too can have an ascended master come into your life to show you your purpose and often you then have a large amount of important work to do within humanity.

What should you do with a spirit guide?

When a spirit guide shows up in your life, it is wise to listen. It is also wiser to discern whether they are in fact a guide or a rampant spirit seeking to cause harm. Asking the intention of your guide is not disrespectful and if it is your guide, it will always be met with a heart-centered answer. If you have indeed made a connection with your spirit guide/s, then it is a wonderful thing to setup an altar or place in your home where you simply acknowledge them and leave them gifts or notes. Do not mistake this with worship. Your spirit guides will never ask you to worship them, and you will never have to. However, it is nice to simply acknowledge them and thank them for their wisdom and guidance.

Having a notebook dedicated to their messages is something that will come in handy even after your guides are gone. A spirit guide notebook that contains all the messages that you receive, from your totems, to your ancestral guides, to the temporary archetypes that come into your life. Sometimes the visions or messages do not make sense at that time but come six months later and you're paging through the book, and a lightbulb goes on setting you onto your right path.

Connecting with spirit is tricky for the human mental filter to consciously grasp. Everyone is not always in *spirit-mode* and if they are, they are usually called flighty or said to have their head in the clouds. It's almost near to impossible to remain in spiritual union 24/7 and for this reason we have our trusty notebooks, our sacred spaces and dedicated sacred time.

The following list is a 'safe' list of spirits and deities that have a compassionate heart toward the human condition and should not cause any malicious acts or harm toward you, so long as you offer the respect and the devotion and as long as your heart is calling them and not an egotistical power driven intention.

Gods for the Neophyte

OILS, RESINS, INCENSES

There are thousands of various incenses, resins and oils on the market today. For the aspiring witch, many of them will be bought and stocked up on, however learning to make them yourself, is by far one of the greatest tools to add to your knowledge box.

One of the best companions for this section in its entirety is Scott Cunningham's *Incense, Oils and Brews*. It never fails one and always has substitutes and warnings when the ingredients are poisonous or if the incense tends to be a little over the top.

Resins and oils are really self-explanatory and do not leave one with much room but to use store bought resins and oils. Incenses on the other hand, leave a lot of room to play. For the sake of beginners, the method below is for loose incense. Whilst making loose incense may seem like a simple one, it is actually a very delicate one.

What you will need:

- A bottle of seed oil.
- Sawdust, wood chips, bark shavings.
- 3 different dried herbs or crushed resin.
- 1 essential oil.
- Self-lighting coals.

Directions:

For the sake of explaining this method, the following recipe will be used:

Divination Loose Incense Recipe

What you will need:

- Holy Basil leaves (1 cup).
- 2 Teaspoons of Sandalwood powder.
- 3 Tears of Frankincense.
- 2 drops of Patchouli essential oil.
- 2 cups of seed oil (Pomace Oil)
- 2 cups of wood chips.

Directions:

- Mix together the dried herbs and the resins. It may be necessary to use a pestle and mortar to crush the resins into a powder. A coffee grinder does work wonders.

- Now add the wood chips to the dried ingredients.

- Into a single cup of seed oil, drop your 2 drops of patchouli oil.

- Now begin pouring the oil mix into the dried mix. The consistency that you are looking for is (when you squeeze it, it must make a stiff ball, however the second you let go it can crumble.)

- Pour the oil until the above consistency is achieved.

- This recipe should last 3 – 4 months.

- When you are done. Light the coal and drop a pinch of your amazing divination incense on the coal, allow it to burn. Drop more as needed.

HERBS, TREES, FLOWERS

Besides the resins, oils and incenses making use of the plants, flowers and trees. We must understand that the plant kingdom is its own world. It has a spirit deva protecting every plant, flower and tree. There is so much magick within the plant kingdom and this is one place that fascinates almost every single witch. There are however many of them who do not make use of the natural world and that is also alright. However, if you choose to use the plant kingdom, make sure that you always show respect to the relevant spirits, and do your homework. Always do your research! Many plants look like others, and whilst the one is a healer the other can be a killer. Also, unless you have a botany background, do not, for the love of the Goddess, go and ingest anything without consulting a doctor.

Do not believe everything that you read on the internet. For a personal story, the shamans where I studied, taught us to diet a plant for a week or longer. This meant no food only water. I took up learning about the deva of Mugwort. Well, a week later it was quite a bloody mess. I had ruptured my intestine from the dose of Mugwort, which was not even that high. However, I learned immediately that the spirit of Mugwort is not kind to the stomach if you overdo it. One cup of Mugwort tea in a 2-week period is fine. Further than that, she is going to go into your body and mess things up. The internet prescribes approximately 3 cups a day. This is ludicrous and an acquaintance who listened to the internet's advice, went ahead, drank 3 -5 cups a day, attempting to strengthen her psychic awareness and what happened was a hospital trip.

On the subject of psychic awareness. You are already in tune with the universe, dear soul, why is it that you feel that if you burn 100 tears of frankincense and drink a field of Mugwort tea that you are going to become more psychic. Your intuition came with the package at birth. It takes practice, not poisoning your system or burning the house down. Besides, anyone who has ever had the psychic visions that I speak of will know, that if they not appearing yet, they will and some days you will wish that you were back in the *hunting for a psychic strength remedy* phase. For the sake of magick, here are a few trees, flowers and herbs for your magickal practice.

MAGICKAL TREES

Birch	New Beginnings
Rowan	Protection against psychic attack
Alder	Stability
Willow	Goddess, Emotions, Harmony, Lunar magick
Ash	Crossing the veil, integration
Hawthorn	The Hag, The underworld

Oak	Stability, The God
Holly	Fatherhood
Hazel	Divination
Apple	Love
Bramble	Learning
Ivy	Perseverance
Blackthorn	Spiritual leadership
Elder	The Goddess
Elm	Healing, third eye
Gorse	Fertility
Heather	Luck
Aspen	To petition death for time
Yew	Transformation
Mistletoe	Truth

Magickal Flowers

Oak flower	Bravery
Gorse flower	Banish depression
White Chestnut flower	Mental clarity
Water Violet flower	Self-confidence
The monkey flower	Release fear
Agrimony flower	Standing in your own truth
Rock Rose	Anxiety
Centaury flower	Inner and outer strength and willpower strength
Knawel flower	Decision making
Policeman's Helmet flower	Harmony and peace
Chicory flower	Release of unwanted people

Vervain flower	Harmony and loosening of thoughts
Old man's beard flower	Stability and grounding
Heather	Combat loneliness
Plumbago flower	Trust and community
Felwort flower	Combating doubt
Olive flowers	Energetic boost
Rock water flower	Relaxation

COMMON MAGICKAL HERBS

Adders Tongue	Healing
Anemone	Protection
Angelica	Exorcism

Balm of Gilead	Love and passion
Benzoin	Purification
Sea Oak	Psychic Power
Hart's Thorn	Legal matters
Swallow Herb	Protection and Happiness
Foxtail	Protection
British Tobacco	Visions
Dragon's Blood Palm	Exorcism, Potency, Love
Holly	Dream magick
High John the Conqueror Root	Success, money
Pearl Moss	Financial abundance
Jacob's Ladder	Mental clarity and control

Summer's Bride	Prophetic Dreams
Maple	Money, luck in gambling
Mizquitl	Healing
Meadow Rue	Divination
Brandy Mint	Psychic powers and prophetic dreams
Wild Senna	Love
Sacred Bark	Legal matters, dispelling quarrels
Palms Christi Root	Protection
Cinchona	Protection
Copal	Purification
English Elm	Love

Ava Root	Visions
Job's Tears	Wishes fulfilled
Mugwort	Prophetic dreams and visions
Shepard's Herb	Divination
Pistachio	Breaking love spells
Dog Grass	Lust and passion
St. John's Wort	Happiness
Moonwort	Open sealed doors
Yerba Louisa	Purification of the self and the home

CRYSTALS AND STONES

Crystals, like herbs, have a vibration, an energetic blueprint that, when placed close to you, will affect your own vibration and energetic system. Sometimes the vibrations take time to take effect because of the emotional baggage that you are carrying and sometimes a certain vibration will work so fast with you that you will not be able to believe your eyes.

Below are some common, easy to find crystals that have a wonderful effect on the human energetic system. Remember that the crystal must call you, and you must feel the pull. This is an old witch's tale, but it does work. Sometimes you only realise why a certain crystal pulled you, months after you purchased it.

Fluorite	Mental clarity and controller of emotions
Garnet	Protection and banishment
Hag Stones	Divination, psychic enhancement and dream work
Hematite	Grounding and protection
Green Jade	Financial prosperity
Red Jasper	For a 'return to sender' effect
Witch's Amber	Divination
Lapis Lazuli	Psychic awareness and divination
Lepidolite	Protection against nightmares
Malachite	Protection (always use in conjunction with a rose quartz)
Mica	Astral projection

Moonstone	Divination and psychic awareness
Obsidian	Protection and grounding
Opal	Astral projection, healing and psychic awareness
Petrified Wood	Past life issues and regressions
Sapphire	Love, power and psychic awareness
Selenite	Reconciliation with old lovers
Sodalite	Wisdom
Topaz	Weight loss
Bloodstone	Spiritual and physical strength

DIVINATION

Divination – the magical art of foretelling future events as well as current events through the use of various tools. Tarot, oracle, playing cards, crystal balls, runes, candles, water, fire, birds, pebbles and bones all use the art of intuition and insight. There is no magic trick involved in divination. There does need to be a certain level of practice behind the person divining and also a 100% level of trust between you and the choice of divination method.

That is all there is to it. Oh, and of course your divine connection. You cannot read without your divine connection. Without the soul in the practice there will be no message for the person receiving the divination. To become good at divining for other people, you need to practice. If tarot is not working for you, try an oracle deck, if that doesn't work, try something else. The secret is the giddy feeling to learn the divination method.

Personally, Tarot, Lenormand, and scrying are my choices for divining. Fire scrying can be one of the most incredible and frighteningly accurate experiences. Water scrying is a little more peaceful and gentler on the soul. The other factor that will come with practicing divination is mediumship. The spirits will begin to talk, sometimes they won't stop and other times they will disappear for months on end.

The important part is that you learn to go with the timing and the flow of your inner soul clock and the clock of the universe. Nothing will ever remain the same, your practice will always change, alter and move into the direction that it needs to be.

Divination is an imagination of the divine game at play. So, choose your method wisely and always use your chosen method with respect and reverence.

Runes of The Elder Futhark

When studying the runes from the Nordic pantheon, it is imperative that you understand the mythology behind the runes. You should also know the deities involved and that each rune is an entire world by itself. The elder futhark is the oldest known magical system. It only became a writing system after the need for communication through a written form, before that it was magic. Each rune, each Aett, each combination is an entire universe, and the runes are not free from teaching lessons.

It is said that the gods still whisper through the symbols and with enough contemplation and devotion you will hear them whisper to you. The runemasters were called Vitki and they were women. Women who carried their runes wherever they went in cat skin pelt pouches.

A Vitki would study a single rune for a year or more, and only once the lessons were done, would the practitioner move on to the next.

Here is the rune poem stating how Odin received the runes. Translated from Old Norse (Aelfric, 2017):

Veit ec at ec hecc vindga meiði a

netr allar nío,

geiri vndaþr oc gefinn Oðin,

sialfr sialfom mer,

a þeim meiþi, er mangi veit, hvers hann af rótom renn.

Við hleifi mic seldo ne viþ hornigi,

nysta ec niþr,

nam ec vp rvnar,

opandi nam,

fell ec aptr þaðan.

I know that I hung on a windy tree

nine long nights,

wounded with a spear, dedicated to Odin,

myself to myself,

on that tree of which no man knows from where its roots run.

No bread did they give me nor a drink from a horn,

downwards I peered;

I took up the runes,

screaming I took them,

then I fell back from there."

For all the rune meanings, studying the Anglo-Saxon rune poems translated by Dickens will help you immensely on your journey. For the sake of this book, only the English translation will be added in.

Feoh

Wealth is a comfort to all men;

yet must every man bestow it freely,

if he wish to gain honour in the sight of the Lord.

Ur

The aurochs is proud and has great horns;

it is a very savage beast and fights with its horns;

a great ranger of the moors, it is a creature of mettle.

Thorn

The thorn is exceedingly sharp,

an evil thing for any knight to touch,

uncommonly severe on all who sit among them.

Os

The mouth is the source of all language,

a pillar of wisdom and a comfort to wise men,

a blessing and a joy to every knight.

Rad

Riding seems easy to every warrior while he is indoors

and very courageous to him who traverses the high-roads

on the back of a stout horse.

Cen

The torch is known to every living man by its pale, bright flame;

it always burns where princes sit within.

Gyfu

Generosity brings credit and honour, which support one's dignity;

it furnishes help and subsistence

to all broken men who are devoid of aught else.

Wynn

Bliss he enjoys who knows not suffering, sorrow nor anxiety,

and has prosperity and happiness and a good enough house.

Haegl

Hail is the whitest of grain;

it is whirled from the vault of heaven

and is tossed about by gusts of wind

and then it melts into water.

Nyd

Trouble is oppressive to the heart;

yet often it proves a source of help and salvation

to the children of men, to everyone who heeds it betimes.

Is

Ice is very cold and immeasurably slippery;

it glistens as clear as glass and most like to gems;

it is a floor wrought by the frost, fair to look upon.

Ger

Summer is a joy to men, when God, the holy King of Heaven,

suffers the earth to bring forth shining fruits

for rich and poor alike.

Eoh

The yew is a tree with rough bark,

hard and fast in the earth, supported by its roots,

a guardian of flame and a joy upon an estate.

Peordh

Peorth is a source of recreation and amusement to the great,
where warriors sit blithely together in the banqueting-hall.

Eolh

The Eolh-sedge is mostly to be found in a marsh;
it grows in the water and makes a ghastly wound,
covering with blood every warrior who touches it.

Sigel

The sun is ever a joy in the hopes of seafarers
when they journey away over the fishes' bath,
until the course of the deep bears them to land.

Tir

Tiw is a guiding star; well does it keep faith with princes;
it is ever on its course over the mists of night and never fails.

Beorc

The polar bears no fruit; yet without seed it brings forth suckers,
for it is generated from its leaves.
Splendid are its branches and gloriously adorned
its lofty crown which reaches to the skies.

Eh

The horse is a joy to princes in the presence of warriors.

A steed in the pride of its hoofs,

when rich men on horseback bandy words about it;

and it is ever a source of comfort to the restless.

Mann

The joyous man is dear to his kinsmen;

yet every man is doomed to fail his fellow,

since the Lord by his decree will commit the vile carrion to the earth.

Lagu

The ocean seems interminable to men,

if they venture on the rolling bark

and the waves of the sea terrify them

and the courser of the deep heed not its bridle.

Ing

Ing was first seen by men among the East-Danes,

till, followed by his chariot,

he departed eastwards over the waves.

So the Heardingas named the hero.

Ethel

An estate is very dear to every man,

if he can enjoy there in his house

whatever is right and proper in constant prosperity.

Dæg

Day, the glorious light of the Creator, is sent by the Lord;
it is beloved of men, a source of hope and happiness to rich and poor,
and of service to all.

Ac

The oak fattens the flesh of pigs for the children of men.
Often it traverses the gannet's bath,
and the ocean proves whether the oak keeps faith
in honourable fashion.

Æsc

The ash is exceedingly high and precious to men.
With its sturdy trunk it offers a stubborn resistance,
though attacked by many a man.

Yr

Yr is a source of joy and honour to every prince and knight;
it looks well on a horse and is a reliable equipment for a journey.

Ior

Iar is a river fish and yet it always feeds on land;

it has a fair abode encompassed by water, where it lives in happiness.

Ear

The grave is horrible to every knight,

when the corpse quickly begins to cool

and is laid in the bosom of the dark earth.

Prosperity declines, happiness passes away

and covenants are broken.

THE TAROT

The tarot we know today is from the great philosophical mind of Edward Arthur Waite. Together with the illustrations from Pamela Colman Smith, we received what is known as the Rider-Waite

Tarot. There are thousands of websites and books promising to teach you the tarot in under 2 hours or in 10 days or some other ludicrous claim. Tarot needs practice and there are 78 cards in a traditional tarot, following the Rider-Waite system, 56 of those are known as the minor arcana, and 22 cards attributed to the major arcana.

The tarot is a story using archetypal imagery, occult symbolism and numerological correspondences to bring an entire universe in a single deck. Some decks that have modern imagery manage to bring this story to life very well, others do not at all. It sounds so boring to begin with a traditional Rider-Waite deck, however when you get into the symbolism and the remarkable amount of information that is contained within each card of the tarot, your interest will be renewed. If it is not, then perhaps tarot is not for you.

If for example you want to learn the tarot but funds are not great, then make sure to visit the website: www.learntarot.com. The author of the book, which is given away for free, and the course and the cheat sheets that we have added below, is Joan Bunning. She has assisted millions of aspiring tarot readers with an excellent point to start their journey, completely free of charge.

The Major Arcana

FOOL (0)	MAGICIAN (1)	HIGH PRIESTESS (2)	EMPRESS (3)
Beginning Spontaneity Faith Apparent Folly	Action Conscious Awareness Concentration Power	Non-Action Unconscious Awareness Potential Mystery	Motherhood Abundance Senses Nature
EMPEROR (4)	HIEROPHANT (5)	LOVERS (6)	CHARIOT (7)
Fatherhood Structure Authority Regulation	Education Belief Systems Conformity Group Identification	Relationship Sexuality Personal Beliefs Values	Victory Will Self-Assertion Hard Control
STRENGTH (8)	HERMIT (9)	WHEEL OF FORTUNE (10)	JUSTICE (11)
Strength Patience Compassion	Introspection Searching Guidance	Destiny Turning Point Movement	Justice Responsibility Decision Cause and

| Soft Control | Solitude | Personal Vision | Effect |

HANGED MAN (12)	**DEATH (13)**	**TEMPERANCE (14)**	**DEVIL (15)**
Letting Go	Ending	Temperance	Bondage
Reversal	Transition	Balance	Materialism
Suspension	Elimination	Health	Ignorance
Sacrifice	Inexorable Forces	Combination	Hopelessness

TOWER (16)	**STAR (17)**	**MOON (18)**	**SUN (19)**
Sudden Change	Hope	Fear	Enlightenment
Release	Inspiration	Illusion	Greatness
Downfall	Generosity	Imagination	Vitality
Revelation	Serenity	Bewilderment	Assurance

JUDGEMENT (20)	**WORLD (21)**
Judgment	Integration
Rebirth	Accomplishment
Inner Calling	Involvement

Absolution   Fulfilment

The Minor Arcana

	WANDS	CUPS	SWORDS	PENTACLES
ACE	Creative Force Enthusiasm Confidence Courage	Emotional Force Intuition Intimacy Love	Mental Force Truth Justice Fortitude	Material Force Prosperity Practicality Trust
TWO	Personal Power Boldness Originality	Connection Truce Attraction	Blocked Emotions Avoidance Stalemate	Juggling Flexibility Fun
THREE	Exploration Foresight Leadership	Exuberance Friendship Communit	Heartbreak Loneliness Betrayal	Teamwork Planning Competence

		y		
FOUR	Celebration Freedom Excitement	Self-Absorption Apathy Going Within	Rest Contemplation Quiet Preparation	Possessiveness Control Blocked Change
FIVE	Disagreement Competition Hassles	Loss Bereavement Regret	Self-Interest Discord Open Dishonour	Hard Times Ill Health Rejection
SIX	Triumph Acclaim Pride	Good Will Innocence Childhood	The Blues Recovery Travel	Having/Not Having: Resources Knowledge Power
SEVEN	Aggression Defiance Conviction	Wishful Thinking Options Dissipation	Running Away Lone-Wolf Style	Assessment Reward Direction

		n	Hidden Dishonour	Change
EIGHT	Quick Action Conclusion News	Deeper Meaning Moving On Weariness	Restriction Confusion Powerlessness	Diligence Knowledge Detail
NINE	Defensiveness Perseverance Stamina	Wish Fulfilment Satisfaction Sensual Pleasure	Worry Guilt Anguish	Discipline Self-Reliance Refinement
TEN	Overextending Burdens Struggle	Joy Peace Family	Bottoming Out Victim Mentality Martyrdom	Affluence Permanence Convention

	WANDS	CUPS	SWORDS	PENTACLES	
PAGE		Be Creative Be Enthusiastic Be Courageous Be Confident	Be Emotional Be Intuitive Be Intimate Be Loving	Use Your Mind Be Truthful Be Just Have Fortitude	Have an Effect Be Practical Be Prosperous Be Trusting/Trustworthy
KNIGHT Positive		Charming Self-Confident Daring Adventurous Passionate	Romantic Imaginative Sensitive Refined Introspective	Direct Authoritative Incisive Knowledgeable Logical	Unwavering Cautious Thorough Realistic Hardworking
KNIGHT		Superficial Cocky	Overemotional	Blunt Overbearin	Stubborn Unadventurous

Negative	Foolhardy Restless Hot-Tempered	Fanciful Temperamental Over refined Introverted	g Cutting Opinionated Unfeeling	Obsessive Pessimistic Grinding
QUEEN	Attractive Wholehearted Energetic Cheerful Self-Assured	Loving Tender-hearted Intuitive Psychic Spiritual	Honest Astute Forthright Witty Experienced	Nurturing Bighearted Down-to-Earth Resourceful Trustworthy
KING	Creative Inspiring Forceful Charismatic Bold	Wise Calm Diplomatic Caring Tolerant	Intellectual Analytical Articulate Just Ethical	Enterprising Adept Reliable Supporting Steady

THE BLACK MIRROR

The black mirror is not a toy, or a tool for those who do not know how to protect their home, their loved ones and themselves. The black mirror is however a strong doorway to the other side or across the veil. It is a *'one witch'* tool, and no one should even know where your black mirror is.

To craft a black mirror, insure that you use a mirror and not just a piece of glass. Follow the instructions below very carefully and use the black mirror in protective circle, always.

What you will need:

- A round mirror
- Black water-proof paint
- A paintbrush
- A few pieces of quartz crystals
- A brick
- A cement place where you can crush the crystal
- A black velvet cloth, big enough to cover the mirror three times
- The Dark moon
- A bag of sea salt

- Candles

Directions:

- Cast circle, making sure you have everything that you need inside the circle.
- Spread sea salt around the perimeter of the circle.
- Repeat the following chant:

"Oh, divine Goddess of the void and black moon,

I seek to access the veil beyond as you do,

Grant me the honour to attune,

To traverse the spiritual landscape beyond the veil,

Through this black mirror I now downscale

The universe as is your domain."

- Now crush the quartz crystal, or if you have crushed it prior to this, then place it to one side.
- Paint the black mirror until the coat is thick and no part of the mirror shows through.
- Sprinkle the clear quartz crystal pieces across the wet paint.
- Now hold your receiving hand to the black moon, and your gifting hand over the black mirror, just like the position of the magician tarot card.

- Repeat the following over and over again until the hair on your body rises up and you know that this mirror has been attuned.

"Attune to,

Black moon,

Black mirror through."

The black mirror is the black or dark moon. At zero percent illumination the void is there for us to see. The dark moon is really used for far more than banishing, but please use it with caution because as Nietzsche said:

"And if you gaze long enough into an abyss, the abyss will gaze back into you."

CRYSTAL BALL GAZING

Crystal ball gazing is a form of scrying. The crystal ball itself has no magical ability. When scrying, what is happening is that the images from your mind's eye are being projected onto a surface. A scryer is able to project his/her images onto any surface of their choosing. However, a crystal ball, made of clear crystal quartz will strengthen and empower the gifts of the practitioner to a percentage that is directly proportionate to the size of the crystal ball.

Many practitioners believe that a glass ball and a crystal ball are the same thing, they are not. A crystal ball has inclusions that show that the ball is in fact made from clear quartz crystal, whereas a glass ball is perfectly clear. If you are fortunate enough to come across a Victorian Era scrying ball, they are made of glass and cut in angular patterns, like how a diamond is cut. These prove to be one of the best devices when choosing to crystal gaze.

The Lunar Calendar

The Dark Moon

The Dark Moon - The time of Cord Cutting Rituals, Infinity Cord Cuttings, Dark Magick that seeks to delve into the separation of anything that does not serve the highest path that you seek. This night is the night of endings to make place for the magick that will happen on the New Moon. This is the night where we seat ourselves alongside the depths of the wisdom held by the Crone and we perform magick of destruction before creation. This is the night of facing the void, crossing the veil, communing with those that have passed on, meditating on the shadow aspects of the self and of our own lives.

This night beckons purification rituals, rituals of banishing and protection, rituals of destruction, magick found in the void, and spell work that hearkens to the darkness within. The Dark Moon, just like the Full Moon is an Esbat of great importance. It should always be prepared for during the waning phase of the moon and every witch can benefit from the workings of Dark Moon magick. Prophetic Magick is also especially potent on the Dark Moon.

Scrying, Tarot Reading, and any other forms of divining are recommended on this night, however, make triply sure that you protect and prepare for what you shall find on the night of the Dark Moon. No magick on this night is for the faint hearted.

Dark Moon Deities: Kali, Hecate, Cerridwen, Morrigan, Badb, Nemain, Hella, Kalma, Lilith, Nephtys.

New Moon

Appearing just after the dark moon, New Moon Magick is where you set the intention, spell good fortune and cast spells of growth, prosperity and health. Even though the actual moons strength is not that great, it is the first sliver of new beginnings. Any magick that incorporates growth, light and positivity are encouraged during this time. The New Moon is also an excellent time for divination into queries of the future aspects of life. It is wise to begin positive spell work during this time and strengthen it toward the full moon where the final working is done.

If you cleansed, banished or performed magick during the waning and Dark Moon then this is really the time to fill the gaps that were emptied. The New Moon provides the witch with a new start. It is the night to begin again. Call on the Maiden and create what you desire. Just like the Sabbats use the Sun, so the Esbats use the moon. Make sure you do not miss this night of powerful magick potential.

Deities to call on: Persephone, Aega, Coyolxauhqui, Kuan Yin, Lasya, Sadarnuna.

Waxing Crescent Moon

The Waxing Crescent is sometimes preferred over the New Moon for starting your spell work, but only because you can actually see the moon up in the night sky. If your magick began on the New Moon, make sure to increase its power by reinforcing the magick throughout the waxing moon until you reach full moon. The Waxing crescent is a time for setting your goals to manifest on the full moon, or in two or three full moons time. It is the time to sew good intentions positively project healing and wellbeing into your life. The entire scope of the Waxing Moon, from the New Moon until the Full Moon is a time of renewal, of second chances and of growth and prosperity. It is a fruitful time, and so should all your magical workings be the same!

Waxing Gibbous Moon

The Waxing Gibbous is a time to project heightened magick into the universe. The power of the moon is great, and influences can be felt quite strongly already. Re-energising and re-affirming your New Moon magick are an excellent idea. It is also a great time to cut your hair, ensuring its speedy growth. Love Magick is also extremely successful if performed during this phase of the lunar wheel.

Financial matters that were dealt with on the new moon, should be revisited and empowered. The waxing Gibbous is a moon of success and the first sign of the mother aspect of the Goddess emerging. It is now a time of working with the Mother, and/or the Maiden aspects in your magick.

Full Moon

The Full Moon, the time of great magick and wish fulfilment. An old tale whispers secrets of how a single heart felt desire spoken out loud to the great Mother in the sky will come true by the time she shows her belly again. This night all magick of growth, of empowerment, of love, of money, of spiritual enlightenment, of mental clarity, direction and receiving is performed. It is a highly important Esbat and a large degree of witches never miss this evening. It is also the evening of performing Drawing Down the

Moon and making healing poppets. It is an especially brilliant night for women or men seeking feminine inspiration to bask in the moonlight and feel the presence of the Goddess.

Scrying on the night of the full moon is something which is always magickal and provides many answers to the seeker without much effort. Protection amulets, mojo bags, healing poppets, witches' besoms, tools of the craft and moon water are all created and blessed upon this especially magickal night. The Mother Goddess is in her full power and she makes it known, many humans feel the effects of the full moon and many of them feel as though they are crawling out of their skins. Witches know how to balance, calm and utilise the full moons energy wisely.

Deities recommended on the full moon: Diana, Cerridwen, Seline, Gwaten, Kuan Yin, Sarpandit, Sefkhet, Rhiannon, Ina, Ishtar, Andromeda, Isis, Ameterasu, Danu, Ernmas, Gaia, Lakshmi, Ma'at, Nuit, Triple Goddess, Shakti, Venus.

Waning Gibbous Moon

The Waning Gibbous is the time to analyse your life. Shadow work begins here. The dark mother aspects are venerated, and we begin to take a good hard look at every aspect of our lives in detail.

Deities to use during the waning moon: Morrigan, Kali Ma, Cerridwen, Macha, Badb, Shakti, Ishtar, Chandi

Last Quarter Moon

The Last Quarter is a stronger dark energy. It is likened to the feeling of bathwater running out whilst you are still in the bath, this is that first pull and heaviness that you feel. The Last Quarter signals the first appearance of the Crone, She and the Dark Mother now lend aid to your magick. It is not yet time to cut cords, but it is time to clean out the unnecessary. It is time to reorganise and to revaluate your life, your modes of thinking, your actions and to go inward. The Last Quarter is excellent for introspection work. The remaining light of the Mother will guide you through your shadow work in a loving manner.

Waning Crescent Moon

The Waning Crescent sees the last of the Dark Mother becoming the Crone, her wisdom now at nearing its peak. Creation of 'Witch Bottles', banishing magick and all manners of cord cuttings can begin being planned for to take place on the Dark Moon. It is a great time to walk the road of the shadow self along-side the Crone. Ask her for wisdom, ask her to reveal in the darkness that which needs to come to the light. Problems which are obscure can be magickly placed before the crone and answers will be found in scrying. The last of the light in the moon lends aid to the darkness and creation of dark altars, veneration to the Crone aspect of the Goddess and the energy within is performed. Hexing can also be performed under this moon, but also remember - with great caution and understand the consequences.

Chapter 5 – Pathworking's for the Witch

The pathworking – Into the Celtic Fray

Breathe in deeply and hold your breath

Now exhale as hard as you can.

Blow out all your frustration, blow out your insecurities, blow out your fear.

Now breathe in deeply again and hold your breath

Blow out all your anxiety, your mistrust, your pain, your anger, your resentment,

Breathe in deeply, hold your breath, close your eyes

Breathe out as hard as you can and relax.

You're standing on the top of a balcony with two marble staircases leading down the left side and the right side. The marble beneath your feet is white with flecks and streaks of black running across its surface. You place your hand at the top of the chrome railing, you feel the coolness beneath your fingertips, you feel the security of its support. You take your first step. The light behind you is luminating the stairs beneath you. The rough rock walls with their striations cause shadows deceiving your eyes. You continue down the spiraling staircase, the warmth of the descent engulfing your being. You take another few stairs down watching the shadows become less as the light begins to dim even more. You can now see the lantern at the bottom of the staircase.

The candlelight brings you a sense of comfort. You feel eager to see what lies ahead. There are a few stairs remaining before the landing where you can just make out the oak door that's copper binds have a green hue from years of ageing. You reach the door. Its handle is a round copper ring. You grab hold of the handle and tug as hard as you can, and the swollen wood gives way. Behind the door are three rough carved stone steps and in the glimmer of the light you can see the spiderwebs, their strands as thick as wool, sticky and glistening in the flickers of light. As you reach forward the webs cling to you, the ever-present thought of what created these lingers in the back of your mind. But nothing living seems to be moving amongst these strands. You press forward grabbing the web and desperately trying to remove it from your body and your clothing.

As you step forward the light seems more and more intense. As you break through the last metre of web, the illuminating moss that covers this cave shines a gentle light on the underground pool of water. Sitting beside it is a hunched figure, staring intently into the reflecting waters. Without turning they acknowledge your presence by lifting their hand and motioning you toward them. They offer you a place by their side on the soft feathery moss. The natural heat of being so deep underground warms your body. The coolness of the spiderwebs no longer seems to concern you. As you stare into the pool of water, the reflection of your new-found guide stares back at you. They slowly slip a wooden tube from within their cloak and place it before you.

You notice that the one end has been closed by a red wax seal. With mere hand gestures they instruct you to remove the seal and you pull an ancient parchment out. As you unroll the parchment, you notice the language upon it is not something you immediately recognize but eventually the lettering forms an image that is so clear in your mind. A message of love, trust, self-worth and pride. In this darkest place you have found the answer to your question. You sit quietly beside your spiritual guide who nods in agreement that you have achieved the lesson that you came here seeking. Once again, they motion you to roll up the parchment and place it back in the tube. They slowly take this from you and push it into your pocket, and silently motion you to leave this place of sanctuary for now. As you turn your head you notice the obstacles that you faced getting here no longer exist.

The passageway of webbing is now open, the candlelight from the oak door illuminates your path back. You notice the rough stone that you tread on, now shines with the footsteps of mother of pearl. The rainbow hue tells you that this is a path that you can come back to tread as often as you desire. The warmth clings to you as you head toward the oak door which is wide open and without obstacles. You slide your feet onto the first of the marble stairs and you notice a faint in the distance above you. You begin ascending the marble staircase, the light now growing stronger and clearer. You begin to recognize the fragrant incense from before.

As you once again reach the balcony you find the people that you love and trust eagerly awaiting the message that you have brought from your guide. They embrace you with love and acceptance knowing that the journey that you have just taken has opened you to the beauty of your own soul and to the beauty of others. The gatekeeper ushers you out slowly snuffing out the candles onto the balcony. The outer door opens, and you see before you a large elder tree and kern. This is your doorway to return always to the Celtic fray. Breathe in deeply and start to feel your physical body. Slowly move your fingers, wiggle your toes, and when you are ready open your eyes.

Without saying a word, write down your experience in your notebook.

Pathworking – Meeting your spirit guides, gods and goddesses through the sand

Breathe in deeply and hold your breath

Now exhale as hard as you can.

Blow out all your frustration, blow out your insecurities, blow out your fear.

Now breathe in deeply again and hold your breath

Blow out all your anxiety, your mistrust, your pain, your anger, your resentment,

Breathe in deeply, hold your breath, close your eyes

Breathe out as hard as you can and relax.

You are on a beach, the waves are lapping over the sand, back and forth, back and forth. Watch the waves cover the sand and make it perfect again. I want you to bend down and begin writing the number 30 on the sand, allow the wave to take it away, now 29, 28… 27, watch how each time the sea water removes the number… write the number 26, 25, 24… watch how the sea dissolves these numbers and how calm you are feeling right now. Write 23 in the sand, watch the wave take it away, 22, 21, 20… again the waves wash away the numbers and leave the sand bare. Now write 19, 18, 17, 16… and again watch the numbers disappear. Write 15, 14, 13, 12, 11… and allow them to be washed away by the cleansing sea water. Write 10, 9, 8, 7, 6, 5… and allow the healing sea water to wash away the numbers, leaving you even calmer than before. Now write 4… and let the number be washed away, 3… and let the number be washed away, 2… and let the number be washed away, 1… and let the number be washed away…

Watch the next wave come in and when it disappears there is a trapdoor in the sand, quickly before the next wave washes it away, open it, climb in and close the trapdoor. The room you find yourself in is lit by candlelight. On the walls there are marking, symbols and shapes, all drawn in red paint. You may go and inspect them if you so wish.

There is an archway on the left side of the room, walk towards it. Before you, in the middle of the archway is a jelly like substance, creating a portal. Step through this substance across the veil and into the land of the spirits, the gods, the goddesses. This is the forgotten land, the holy land. In front of you is an entire array of structures. There is a being sitting on a chair in front of these structures. Go toward this being. Look at them intently. Are they motioning anything? Remember their clothing, their face, their hair, their eyes.

They are holding a black box on their lap. They give you the box. You take it and open it. Look at the gift inside. This is the one gift that you need at this moment in your life. Thank the being for the gift. Ask the being to reveal to you a being that you can call on for help during this phase of your life. As you ask this, another being walks up to you. Remember their clothes, their hair, their facial features and anything specific about them that stands out. The second being speaks to you, listen to what they have to say – (Long Pause) – Thank both beings for their time. There is a paper on the floor with a pencil, pick it up and give it to the second being, ask them to write their name on the paper, take the paper and look at the name, remember it. It makes sense to you, and you know this being. Thank them both again. Turn around and see the beach in the distance. Walk toward the sea. When you get to the ocean, allow the waves to lap over your feet. Feel the cold, refreshing water cleanse your feet and know that you are always welcome here.

Smell the incense in the room. Allow yourself to return to your body. Wiggle your toes, your fingers and scrunch your nose. When you are ready open your eyes and write down everything that you have experienced even if you think it makes no sense, it will in time.

Chapter 6 – Using Ritual?

A Basic Standard Wiccan Ritual

"Smudge all who are present before entering the circle.

Anoint all who are present inside the circle area.

Both High Priestess and High Priest kneel before the altar.

Priestess places bowl of water on pentacle, places tip of Athame in water and says:

"I cleanse and consecrate and bless thee O creature of Water that you may be fit to dwell in our sacred Space. In the Names of The Lady of the Moon and the Lord of the Wild, I cleanse, bless and consecrate thee. So, mote it be."

All respond:

"So, mote it be."

The High Priestess replaces the water bowl. The High Priest places the bowl of salt on the pentacle, places tip of Athame in it and says:

"I bless thee O creature of Earth that you may be fit to dwell in our sacred space. In the Names of The Lady of the Moon and the Lord of the Wild, I consecrate and bless thee. So, mote it be."

All respond:

"So, mote it be."

The High Priestess now picks up the water bowl and holds it up with both hands at eye level. The High Priest takes a little salt on the Athame or in hand and drops it into the water, then stirs anticlockwise with finger or Athame saying:

"Water and Earth combined – blessed be"

All respond:

"Blessed Be."

Bowls are returned to their places. High Priestess picks up the Incense burner, adds incense, points Athame at coals and says:

"I cleanse and consecrate and bless thee O creature of Fire that you may be fit to dwell in our sacred Space. In the Names of The Lady of the Moon and the Lord of the Wild, I cleanse, bless and consecrate thee. So, mote it be."

All respond:

"So, mote it be."

The High Priest points Athame at smoke rising from burner and says:

"I cleanse and consecrate and bless thee O creature of Air that you may be fit to dwell in our sacred Space. In the Names of The Lady of the Moon and the Lord of the Wild, I cleanse, bless and consecrate thee. So, mote it be."

All respond:

"So, mote it be."

The High Priestess now combines the fire and air and says:

"Fire and Air combined – blessed be."

All respond:

"Blessed Be."

CIRCLE CASTING DONE BY HIGH PRIESTESS

"I conjure thee O circle of Power that you may serve as a meeting place of love, joy and truth. To serve as a barrier between the world of men and the mighty ones. Keeping out all that is bane and containing all that is of love. To serve as a vessel and focus of the Intent of all gathered here. In the names of The Lady of the Moon and the Lord of the Wild, I conjure thee."

High Priestess picks up the water and salt mixture and walks the circle saying:

"With Water and Earth, I cleanse, bless and consecrate this place that it may be fit to serve as sacred space."

The High Priestess places the bowl back on the Altar. The High Priest picks up Incense burner and walks the circle saying:

"With Fire and Air, I cleanse, bless and consecrate this place that it may be fit to serve as sacred space."

The High Priest then places the burner back on the Altar, they both turn to the coven / group or if solitary just out loud and say:

"The circle is cast, and we are between worlds, where night and day, joy and sorrow, life and death, meet as one. So, mote it be."

All respond:

"So, Mote it be."

Universal Invocation

"Hearken to my call, all which was, is and will be. I call the all-knowing, all seeing Universal Soul, that from which everything comes came and to which everything must return. Come! Enter every heart and mind in this circle, uplifting each individual Spirit to join, for a moment in time, with the All. Hail and Welcome the Universal!"

The Element of Air

"Lords and Ladies of the watchtowers of the East, Elemental Spirits of Air, I do summon, stir and call thee. Bring to our circle your insight and protection and bear witness to our rites. Hail and welcome!"

The Element of Fire (S.H) The Element of Earth (N.H)

"Lords and Ladies of the watchtowers of the North/South, Elemental Spirits of Fire, I do summon, stir and call thee. Bring to our circle your courage and protection and bear witness to our rites. Hail and welcome!"

The Element of Water

"Lords and Ladies of the watchtowers of the West, Elemental Spirits of Water, I do summon, stir and call thee. Bring to our circle your love and protection and bear witness to our rites. Hail and welcome!"

The Element of Earth (S.H.) The Element of Fire (N.H)

"Lords and Ladies of the watchtowers of the South/North, Elemental Spirits of Earth, I do summon, stir and call thee. Bring to our circle your strength and protection and bear witness to our rites. Hail and welcome!"

Invocation of the Goddess done by the High Priestess

The invocation is specific to the ritual. It depends on which Goddess has been chosen or if a general invocation the Goddess is applicable.

Invocation of the God done by the High Priest

The invocation is specific to the ritual. It depends on which Goddess has been chosen or if a general invocation the Goddess is applicable.

Statement of intent. This is the intention of the ritual explained to all who are present in the ritual and what part each person will play.

In a standard Wiccan ritual, a mini form of the Great Rite is used to bless the cakes and ale:

The Cakes and Ale are consecrated. The High Priest kneels in front of the Altar facing the High Priestess. He holds the chalice of ale or fruit juice up to her. She lowers her athame held in both hands, point downwards into the wine while she says:

"As the athame is to the male, so the cup is to the female; and conjoined, they bring fruitfulness and blessings; they become One in truth."

To consecrate the cakes, the High Priestess kneels before the High Priest, holding up the plate of cakes before him. The High Priest traces an invoking pentagram in the air over the cakes and says:

"Oh, Queen most secret, bless this food unto our bodies, bestowing health, wealth, strength, joy and peace and that fulfilment of love which is perfect happiness."

The High Priestess replaces the plate on Altar.

OFFERING LIBATION

The High Priestess and the High Priest make the offering to the Gods.

The High Priestess holds the cup up to eye level and says:

"As all things proceed to us from the Goddess and the God, so must some return to them in recognition of their love and favour. For the Gods and we are each dependent upon the other, and all must have their due. Blessed Be!"

All respond:

"Blessed Be!"

The High Priest holds up the plate to eye level and says:

"Oh, gentle Goddess of the Moon and Lord of Death and Rebirth, accept this token not as a sacrifice, but as token rendering of our appreciation, our love and our respect. Blessed Be!"

All respond:

"Blessed Be!"

Give Libation into the cauldron / bowl that you have set aside for this purpose, it will be given to the earth when the ritual is completed.

Both the High Priestess and the High Priest now share the chalice of ale and the cakes in perfect love and perfect trust. The High Priestess turns to her coven and says:

"We now share fellowship of the soul with one another and the gods."

The High Priest takes the plate and the High Priestess takes cup and they move anti-clockwise around the circle. They take the cakes and ale to each coven member in turn and offer saying:

"I offer you this cup/cakes in perfect love and perfect trust."

The coven member sips the ale or eats the cakes and says:

"I accept in perfect love and perfect trust. Blessed Be."

Once the cakes and ale have been completed the entire circle is taken down, entities are dismissed and bid farewell. This process is as follows:

THE RELEASE OF THE UNIVERSAL SPIRIT

"I thank the Seen and the Unseen, the All, for your presence and love in our circle this night. Leave with us that feeling of connection, oneness that you bring to our souls. I ask that you continue to touch our lives every day. Hail the Universal!"

Dismissal of the Goddess done by The High Priestess

Dismissal of the God done by The High Priest

DISMISSAL OF THE ELEMENT OF EARTH (S.H)

THE ELEMENT OF FIRE (N.H)

"Lords and Ladies of the watchtowers of the South/North, Elemental Spirits of Earth, I do thank thee for bringing your strength and protection to our circle tonight. Hail and farewell!

DISMISSAL OF THE ELEMENT OF WATER

"Lords and Ladies of the watchtowers of the West, Elemental Spirits of Water I do thank thee for bringing your love and protection to our circle tonight. Hail and farewell."

DISMISSAL OF THE ELEMENT OF FIRE (S.H) THE ELEMENT OF EARTH (N.H)

"North Lords and Ladies of the watchtowers of the North/South, Elemental Spirits of Fire, I do thank thee for bringing your courage and protection to our circle tonight. Hail and farewell."

DISMISSAL OF THE ELEMENT OF AIR

"Lords and Ladies of the watchtowers of the East, Elemental Spirits of Air, I do thank thee for bringing your insight and protection to our circle tonight. Hail and farewell."

Release Circle

Ritual is done. Feasting and other grounding exercises can now be done."

WHY BUILD ON THE STANDARD WICCAN RITUAL?

The standard Wiccan ritual is a ritual devised by Gerald B. Gardner, it has been modernised by the Gardnerian lineage covens and altered to suit a modern world. The standard ritual is laid out as it is to ensure that there is a perfect balance throughout the ritual. It ensures that all bases are covered for cleansing, protection and provides the neophyte practitioner a safe space within which to practice their workings.

The standard Wiccan ritual requires nothing, but your own *'theme'* attached to it and the change of deities and attributes requested from the elemental guardians. Ritual architects such as Doreen Valiente, who was most probably responsible for the skeleton edit of this ritual, know how to ensure that there is balance throughout. If you wish to write your own ritual and change the order of the ritual mentioned above, then by all means do so, however, you will notice that the balance may be a little out, or you are left feeling *'off'* after ritual.

Even though the above ritual is a coven ritual outline, the exact same applies in a one-man ritual. The only difference will be that you will have to do all the work yourself.

A NON-WICCAN NORDIC RITUAL WITH PRE-
RITUAL TALK AND EXPLANATION

Pre-Ritual Talk and Explanation

The old Norse way was very different to our own understanding of the world of the gods today. In the ritual journey that we will embark on in an hour or so, we will be joined with the gods in the old ways. We will see them through the gifts of wisdom known as the runes. We will be invoking the man-god who gave his mundane sight for the sight of the gods and through his own journey he, himself became a god. Not many who follow the old ways believe that the great Odin was a human like you and me, but the fact is that each and every one of you have the gods within you. You have the potential to follow the same path to enlightenment just like Odin did.

Odin, it is said, in the poetic sagas and edda's (which are considered as holy texts to those who follow the old norse ways) speak of Odin hanging on Yggdrasil (the old Norse world tree) for nine days and nine nights. It says that no one fed him mead or gave him bread, this leads us to believe that he either suffered the fasting out of his own will or it was done to him. During this time, right before death he was given the wisdom of the magic of the runes. These are known as the elder futhark. The runes have been changed much and today we have a younger futhark, we have a gothic set, we have the Germanic runes and even those Icelandic variations.

Odin returned from his ordeal / journey with only one eye. This, I personally believe is more of a metaphor, in other words he gave up the mundane sight for the spiritual sight. So, he had the runes, he had travelled through the nine worlds of Yggdrasil and he had survived. He passed this knowledge on to worthy rune readers, which I might add, were mostly women. Men were not seen by the Nords as possessing the gifts of fortune telling and women travelled in groups of nine plus one from town to town practicing the art of Seidhr. This is a form of trance. These women were known as Volva's and Their runes were kept on red strings on their belts in cat skins and they provided valuable advice and direction to the people. It was only through Germanic influence that men became bearers of the rune knowledge and were known as Runemasters.

In our ritual, each one of you will be given a set of runes. In our first working we will charge our bag of runes; we will have them charged and consecrated by the old gods and we will set our intentions on them. It is imperative that this bag of runes never be touched by another and never read for anyone but yourself. These are your personal tools and must never be given away, when you have given the study of them up, then bury them deep in mother earth and they will be cleansed until found by another or returned through rot back into the earth.

In our second working we will draw a rune from the bag of odins runes. This rune that you pick will answer a question that you ask and will give you direction. The HP and HPS will lead you through deciphering the message. This rune has a hole for you to wear for the duration of the time its guidance is needed. Again, this amulet is yours alone. When the time comes, and you will feel it, you will bury it and allow its magic to return to the earth.

Now, we also invoke Frigga, Odin's wife or divine consort. She is the mother of the Nordic way, she is the divine aspect of all motherhood, and she overseas fairness and fertility, marriage and all of the gods. She is also the goddess of Seidhr. She will be the balance in the ritual. She will bring the unity required and she will bring the divine influence and gentleness out of Odin. Odin is an ancient energy – he is taken lightly by many, but a wise shamanic energy like his is never stable. It is Frigga who balances him and who channels this divinity from him without the necessary need for any sacrifice.

On the subject of sacrifice, for cakes and ale, it was customary to have a boar slaughtered in Odin's honour. Instead of an entire boar we will have a holy bread baked in the old way. This bread and these cakes and ale will seal the bond between you and the old gods in perfect love and perfect trust.

Any questions?

Let us robe up and go journey with the gods…

Ritual

Robed and ready.

Ritual space is cleansed.

Hold hands.

Grounding

Take up magical identity

Stand and breathe.

Chant softly: "Gods within, divinity awakening"

Both the person who will be anointing and the person who will be smudging will go into circle with HPS and smudge, anoint and then fetch HP smudge and anoint.

Rest of group is smudged and anointed and enters ritual space.

HPS and HP kneel before the altar.

Pentacle is turned upright.

HPS: Bowl of water on pentacle, athame in bowl of water. Says:

"I cleanse and consecrate thee, oh, creature of water, that you may be fit to dwell in sacred space. In the names of Odin and Frigga, I cleanse, bless and consecrate thee. So, mote it be."

All present repeat: *"So mote it be"*

HPS lifts water bowl to eye-level and HP takes a pinch of salt and says:

"Water and Earth combined. Blessed be"

All present repeat: *"Blessed be."*

HPS lights candle with flameage. Points athame at the fire and says:

"I cleanse and consecrate thee, oh creature of fire that you may be fit to dwell in this sacred space. In the names of Odin and Frigga, I cleanse, bless and consecrate thee. So, mote it be."

All those present repeat: *"So mote it be."*

HP picks up the incense burner lights the incense from the flame of the blessed candle and motioning to the smoke says:

"I cleanse, consecrate and bless thee, oh creature of air, that you may be fit to dwell in our sacred space. In the names of Odin and Frigga, I cleanse, consecrate and bless thee, Oh creature of air. So, mote it be."

All who are present repeat: *"So mote it be."*

The HPS now lifts the incense, and says:

"Fire and air combined. Blessed be."

All who are present repeat: *"Blessed be."*

Get ready for circle casting:

Circle of members in the middle. Facing outward. Hum "Om"

HPS casts circle:

"I conjure thee, oh circle of power, that you may serve as a meeting place of love, joy and truth. You are cast to serve as a barrier between the world of men and the mighty ones. Keeping out all that is bane and keeping in all that is of love. You are cast to serve as a vessel and a focus of all the intent of each individual gathered here. In the names of Odin and Frigga, I conjure thee, oh circle of power.

HPS cleanses the circle. Picks up water and salt / Holy water and walks widdershins saying:

"With water and earth combined, I cleanse... bless... and consecrate this space that it may be fit to serve as sacred space."

HP empowers the circle. Picks up the incense burner with incense and walks widdershins saying:

"With fire and air combined, I empower and strengthen this circle, that it may be fit to serve as sacred space."

Both HP and HPS stand at the altar and declare:

"The circle is cast. We are between worlds, where night and day, joy and sorrow, life and death, meet as one. So, mote it be."

All present repeat: *"So mote it be."*

All present make circle in centre of the circle and hands on top of one another holding, trusting and leaning outward. The four callers of the universal standing at the four points in the circle.

Universal invocation shared between four:

"Hearken to my call, all that was, that is, that will be. I call the all-knowing, all seeing, Universal soul, that from which everything comes, came and that to which everything must return. Come! Enter every heart and mind in this circle, uplifting each spirit to join for a moment in time with the All. Hail and Welcome the Universal Spirit."

All present repeat: *"All Hail the Universal Spirit of the All."*

EAST invocation of Air

"Lords and Ladies, of the watchtowers of the EAST, elemental spirits of Air, I do summon, stir and call thee. Bring to our circle your clarity,

insight and protection and bear witness to our rites. Hail and welcome Air."

All present repeat: *"Hail and Welcome Air."*

NORTH invocation of FIRE

"Lords and Ladies of the watchtowers of the NORTH, elemental spirits of FIRE, I do summon, stir and call thee. Bring to our circle your courage to face the unknown and your desire to venture into the void of possibility, bring with you your protection and bear witness to our rites. Hail and welcome FIRE."

All present repeat: *"Hail and Welcome FIRE."*

WEST invocation of WATER

"Lords and Ladies of the watchtowers of the WEST, elemental spirits of WATER, we do summon, stir and call thee. Bring to our circle your perfect love and perfect trust and your protection and bear witness to our rites. Hail and welcome WATER."

All present repeat: *"hail and welcome WATER"*

SOUTH invocation of EARTH

"Lords and Ladies of the watchtowers of the SOUTH, elemental spirits of EARTH, we do summon, stir and call thee. Bring to our circle your stability, your direction and your intertwined connection to Yggdrasil and

bring also your protection and bear witness to our rites. Hail and welcome Earth."

All present repeat: *"Hail and welcome Earth."*

HPS now invokes Goddess aspect Frigga:

"Friiiiigggggaaaaaa, Friiiigggggaaaaaa, Friiiiigggggaaaaaa… Mother of many, seer beyond the realms of gods and men. Bosom holding all beyond time and space. Mother of the gods see into our hearts this night. See into our souls. Mother Frigga we call on you to enter into this sacred space prepared for you and your consort. Join us. Hail and Welcome Mother Frigga."

All Present repeat: *"Hail and Welcome Mother Frigga."*

HP now invokes God aspect Odin:

"Odin… Ooooooh….dddddd…iiii…nnnnn… Odin! Come down from Asgardr, come down to join us in celebrating and learning your wisdom that you hung on Yggdrasil for. Come lend your wisdom to our workings, come lend your sight to our souls. Join your consort Mother Frigga in our sacred space prepared for you this night. Hail and welcome great father Odin!"

All present repeat: *"Hail and welcome Great Father Odin."*

All seated.

HPS now speaks:

"Welcome dear ones. We are now between worlds and joined in sacred space by our Great Father Odin and Great Mother Frigga and the elemental spirits of the four quarters. This is sacred space, and this is safe space. Tonight, we will be given wisdom from the gods. Each one of you will be handed a pouch of runes. They are a gift from the gods. For our first working we will take up the runes in our hands and we will hold them for a while, making a connection with them. You also have a paper in your bag with general guidelines to the meanings of each rune. Do not read the paper, simply place your hands on your runes and feel them. This will be done in silence. We will then charge them by raising energy to the chant of "Gods within, divinity awakening." The chant will peak at awakening. Our second working will be direction from the gods. The HP and HPS will come around and you will ask either HP (Odin) or HPS (Frigga) for direction, guidance. You will then be picking a rune from the bag and either HP or HPS will offer guidance. This rune that you pick will be an amulet for you to hang around your neck. After your guidance is received and everyone has had their chance you will be handed a string and we will then charge the amulet with the chant: "Gods decree, so it shall be" peaking at "it shall be."

Working is done.

Cone is handled both times by HPS. Intentions for first workings are sent into the bags of the members present. Intentions of second working into the amulets. Excess sent into the earth.

Cakes and ale.

Mini Great Rite performed by HP and HPS:

HP holds chalice up to the HPS kneeling before her. The HPS holds the athame up and places it into the chalice whilst proclaiming:

"As the athame is to the male, so the cup is to the female, and conjoined, they bring fruitfulness and blessings, they become one in truth."

HPS kneels before the HP and holds the cakes up to him… in this case it will be the boar bread on a wooden board. He proclaims:

"Oh, queen most sacred, bless this holy boar baked for the gods unto our bodies, bestowing, health, wealth, strength and peace and that fulfilment of love which is perfect happiness."

HPS holds the chalice to eye level and proclaims:

"As all things proceed to us from the goddess and god, so must some return to them in recognition for their love and favour. For the gods and we are each dependent upon each other. All must have their due. Blessed be."

HPS gives libation in the cauldron

All present repeat: *"Blessed be."*

HP holds the cakes up to eye-level and proclaims:

"Oh, gracious goddess Frigga, and mighty father Odin, accept this token not as a sacrifice but as a token rendering our appreciation, our love and our respect. Blessed be!"

HP gives libation in cauldron.

All present repeat *"Blessed be"*

HPS and HP share mead and boar bread in perfect love and perfect trust.

HPS proclaims to coven: *"We now share fellowship of the soul with one another and the gods."*

HP and HPS move widdershins offering cakes and ale in perfect love and perfect trust.

"I offer you this sacred boar bread / mead in perfect love and perfect trust. Blessed be."

Each member responds with:

"I accept this sacred boar bread / mead in perfect love and perfect trust. Blessed be."

Release energies:

Universal Released.

"I thank the seen and the unseen, the All, for your presence and love in our circle this night. Leave with us that feeling of connection and oneness that you bring to our souls. I ask that you continue to touch our lives every day. Hail the Universal"

***(no farewell as the universal is within us always.)

God released by HP

"Great Father Odin we thank you for your sight, your wisdom and your loving guidance. Stay with us on our journeys through Yggdrasil and in our pathways if we choose to pursue the knowledge that your runes hold. For now, we bid you farewell. Hail and Farewell Great Father Odin!"

All present repeat: *"hail and Farewell Great Father Odin."*

HPS releases Goddess aspect

"Divine Mother Frigga, we thank you for bringing your gentleness into our rites and for guiding the energies and the flow of wisdom. Guide us in the future if we choose to pursue the knowledge that the runes hold. For now, we bid you farewell. Hail and farewell Great Mother Frigga."

All present repeat: *"Hail and Farewell Great Mother Frigga."*

SOUTH dismissing EARTH

"Lords and Ladies of the watchtowers of the SOUTH, elemental Spirits of Earth, I do thank thee for bringing your stability, your direction and your intertwined connection to Yggdrasil as well as your protection. Hail and Farewell EARTH."

All present repeat: "Hail and Farewell EARTH."

WEST dismissing WATER

"Lords and Ladies of the watchtowers of the WEST, elemental spirits of Water, I do thank thee for bringing your perfect love and perfect trust and your protection. Hail and Farewell Water."

All present repeat: "hail and farewell Water."

NORTH dismissing FIRE

"Lords and Ladies of the watchtowers of the NORTH, elemental spirits of FIRE. I do thank thee for bringing your courage to face the unknown and your desire to venture into the void of possibility, as well as your protection. Hail and farewell FIRE!"

All present repeat: "hail and farewell Fire."

EAST dismissing Air.

"Lords and Ladies of the watchtowers of the EAST, elemental spirits of Air, I thank thee for bringing your clarity, your insight and your protection. Hail and farewell Air."

All present repeat: *"Hail and farewell air."*

Release the circle.

Enjoy the feasting like a Nordic Warrior.

Chapter 7: Spell work

Today, there is a spell for everything. From getting a new boyfriend, besides the spells to get rid of current ones, there are spells to change your eye colour and to lose weight. The line between reality and hopefulness is very thin, and there is the humour in it all, magic is everywhere. Let me use an example: If you say to yourself, "I have a headache." And you do this for the next 15 – 30 minutes. You will without a doubt end up with a headache or a raging migraine. It depends on your level of imagination, your intention, focus and the strength of your willpower.

Now no-one wants a migraine! So why can the same principle not apply to a million dollars? The answer is that it can. The secret is that you know beyond a shadow of a doubt that you are worth the migraine, capable of receiving a migraine, and that a migraine is a very possible thing. The million dollars has only been a wishful thinking episode and perhaps left to the things of daydreams. There are so many blockages in the mind concerning money, love and health that we think that magic is only for those gifted in the occult arts. It is not. Everyone practices magic every single day. All you have to do is to believe. You need to believe it so hard that your subconscious mind begins to program your daily life onto the path of success, of healing and you need to distance yourself from the non-believers, the ones who will not support your goal. This is also why the witch's pyramid has "to keep silent." At the end.

We are all subject to being mentally changed by the world around us. If your desire is great but your environment does not support this desire, its best you either silence yourself and let no one know about the magic that you are working, or you change your environment to suit your desire. You need to understand that everything that you read, everything that you listen to, everything that you subject yourself to does alter your life to run in line with that. Why would you purposefully subject your life to a situation or to people who do not have your best interests at heart? You wouldn't. So, why do so many people do it? They do it because of fear. You will never achieve a single successful spell if you have doubt or fear. There needs to be absolute trust in the power of the universe and absolute trust in the power you hold inside of you to change whatever it is that you are willing to change.

To quote Frank Herbert:

"I must not fear. Fear is the mind-killer. Fear is the little death that brings total obliteration. I will face my fear. I will permit it to pass over me and through me. And when it has gone past, I will turn the inner eye to see its path. Where the fear has gone there will be nothing. Only I will remain."

Remember this quote, for this is exactly what fear is. Fear nothing and you will accomplish great things. What is stopping you from the greatest success that you can dream of?

SPELLS FOR LOVE

A charm bag to draw love to you

What you will need:

- A square piece of rose red cloth
- A sprig of Rosemary
- A pinch of Orris Root
- A handful of Caraway seeds
- A pinch of Cinnamon
- A photograph, item or piece of hair from the person you are wishing to attract.
- The waxing moon phase.
- A large white board to work on.
- Red String.

Directions:

- Place everything together on the white board. Place the items neatly next to each other and then place both your hands palms facing downward over the items.
- Repeat the following:

"In the name of The Lord and The Lady,

In the great name of love,

I activate, empower and charge each item with drawing intimacy,

With drawing divine passion mirrored above."

- Now place the caraway seeds, the cinnamon, the orris root and the sprig of rosemary into the red square.
- Take the hair or the photograph of the one you have your eye on and close your fist, hold it to your heart and repeat the following as many times as you feel is necessary:

"By the grace of the powers that be,

You shall love me eternally."

- Place their hair or the photograph on top of the items in the red square.
- Fold the four corners together so that you can make a pouch.
- Tie this pouch with red string and whilst you do this repeat the following:

"Love to me, come fast and swift,

By full moon next you shall give me the gift,

Of a lover's heart, of a lover's soul,

Our divine union made to last, mine to be the control."

Carry this pouch on your person and when you see the one you have your eye on, do not be shy, speak to them and make sure to use a sentence with the word union in it. It does not matter how you use the word. Just make sure it is said.

A lover's quarrel box

What you will need:

- A small black box.
- Sheets of white square paper.
- The quarrel.
- A red pen.

Directions:

- Write down the quarrel or the disagreement that you have had with your partner on the white piece of paper.
- Fold the paper as many times as you can and whilst you are folding it, repeat the following:

"Smaller and smaller, quarrel away,

Gone to the wind, forgotten today,

Once I toss you in the void,

Gone you will be until the end of my days."

- Throw the folded quarrel into the black box and let that box be the place where you place any quarrels or disputes, arguments or problems.

The Cowrie Full Moon Baby Boomer

The origin of this spell is unknown; however, it has been passed down through the line of witches and works every time there is someone that has difficulty in falling pregnant.

What you will need:

- 23 Cowrie shells – the small ones are fine.
- 99% illuminated full moon, and the night of the 100% illuminated full moon.
- Your partner.
- Money to buy one pair of booties.
- 2 pieces of your hair, 2 pieces of your partners hair.
- Red string.

Directions:

- Before attempting a steamy night, it would be necessary to set everything up first.

- Place the cowrie shells under the bed in the figure 8 eternity symbol. Make sure that you do this on the first full moon night. It is the second night of the full moon or 100% illumination that your baby will be conceived.

- Once you have placed the cowrie shells in their pattern, walk the figure 8 on all sides of the bed, do this as many times as you can, place both your hands on your womb and repeat:

"A soul I draw to me, open I am, child come to me, mother I am."

- Now go immediately and purchase a pair of baby booties. In the one bootie place your hair, in the other place your partners hair, tie them both together with the red string. Repeat the following as you do so:

"Welcome little one, made from dad and mom, a soul so precious, my own to be, a soul so precious, the time to give life to the seed."

- Place the booties in the middle of the figure 8 under the bed. Make sure it will be undisturbed until you and your partner make love.

SPELLS FOR ABUNDANCE

An Abundant Home Spell.

What you will need:

- 13 fresh peppermint leaves.
- 2 sticks of Cinnamon
- Boiling Water
- A blue bucket
- A mop or a cloth if you will be cleaning on your hands and knees.

Directions:

- **Place the peppermint leaves into the bucket one by one, repeating the following:**

"Peppermint, fresh and inviting, bring to me the abundance so exciting."

- Add the cinnamon sticks into the bucket and repeat the following:

"Cinnamon sights set on gold, bring in riches young and old."

- Add the boiling water on top of the ingredients and allow to steep for 3 minutes. When done, top up with cold water.

- Mop the house now from the front door to the back door walking backwards, whilst you do this hum this chant like a little tune:

"Welcome in abundant things, welcoming you in, welcome in a life of kings, welcoming you in."

- Repeat this spell once in every waxing lunar phase, make sure you do this spell on the waxing moon only.

There's Always Money in My Wallet Spell

What you will need:

- Cinnamon essential oil
- A blue candle
- Any amount of money, it must be a note, not coins.

- Your wallet

Directions:

- Take the note / paper money and rub cinnamon oil on it. Repeat the following:

"Money, money attract more of you, copied and doubled and tripled to hoard.

Money, Money, attract more of you, there is nothing I cannot afford."

- Carry on repeating the chant above as you light the candle. Drip the wax onto the note, three drops of wax are enough.
- Carry on repeating the chant as you place the note into your wallet.

Watch the money multiply!

A Spell of Happiness

What you will need:

- Yourself
- A paper
- A pen
- A rubbish bin

Directions:

- Write down the sadness, all of it, pull it from your mind and allow it to flaw through your arm into the ink and onto the paper.

- Write down everything that you are sad about, and if you do not know why you are sad, do not stress, just write.

- When you are done, you may be feeling a little tired.

- Take up the paper, hold it to the sky and repeat the following chant:

"Depro paper, keeper of that soot in mind, be gone with you, terrible swine!"

- Tear the paper into tiny pieces, be aggressive about it.

- Take a nap. This step is just as important as the ones before. When you wake you will feel much better!

Spells for Health and Healing and Protection

Creating your own protection mojo bag

herbs, crystals and items that signify your guardians or those you trust to protect you are used in gris-gris or mojo bags. A mojo bag is a combination of items that work together to serve a single purpose. In magick the saying, "keep it simple stupid" really works. So today we will be making a powerful protection bag.

What you will need:

- 3 herbs for protection
- 1 essential oil for protection
- 1 crystal for empowerment.

- A square piece of black cloth (black for absorbing negativity)
- Spit / a bit of your hair / a fingernail clipping
- Red ribbon / string
- 1 black candle

Create your sacred space, burn some sage or other cleansing herbs to cleanse your space and ready it for your work. Remember to always cast circle and call in the spirit guides and deities if you have forged such a relationship. Light your black candle and begin your working.

Use the chant below to empower each item that will be added to your mojo bag. Add each one into the bag and then close your bag by folding the four corners together.

Chant:

"Creature of perfection and power,

I call on your ability to protect and empower,

_____, I awaken your protective vibration this instant,

Make me (or another if you are making it for someone else) resistant,

Protect me, shield me, shield all that I hold dear,

Far or near,

Protect and diffuse any negativity,

As I will, so mote it be!"

Take your red string and spin it tightly around the bag to secure it, leaving enough for the nine knots mentioned below. Visualise the powerful protection emanating from the mojo bag. Begin knotting the red string and with each knot follow the rhythm of the following chant, repeating the words as you tie the knots.

"By the knot of one, this spell has begun
By the knot of two, my words are true
By the knot of three, it comes to be
By the knot of four, powerful protection in this core
By the knot of five, the spell is alive
By the knot of six, the spell is fixed
By the knot of seven, this power is now driven
By the knot of eight, all harm now dissipates
By knot of nine, complete protection is mine!"

Take your magickal protection bag and bury it at your front gate / front door in a pot plant or keep it on your person.

The Draining of Negativity Spell

What you will need:

- A bath
- Lavender Oil
- Valerian Tea
- Yourself

Directions:

- This spell can be done without the tea and the lavender; however, these two plants help immensely in this spell. It is effective by itself as well.
- Run enough water to cover your body.
- Drop 4 drops of Lavender essential oil into the bathwater.
- Climb into the bath.
- Valerian is known as the confidante in the herbal kingdom's deva properties, whilst you lie in the water, tell the valerian deva all your pains, your angers, your frustrations. Everything and sip the tea each time.
- When you are done, pull the plug out.
- Lie flat in the water.
- Feel the tug of the water as it drains out of the bath.
- See the negativity leave, down the drain!

Repeat this spell whenever you feel the need to.

DRAWING DOWN THE MOON FOR THE SOLITARY PRACTITIONER

What is Drawing Down the Moon?

Drawing Down the Moon, or alternatively Drawing Down the Goddess is both a practice taken by a High Priestess within ritual in the bounds of circle, or a ritual practice on its own performed by a solitary practitioner.

> *"I am the womb: **of every holt**, I am the blaze: **on every hill**,*
> *I am the queen: **of every hire**,*
> *I am the shield: **for every head**, I am the tomb: **of every hope**."*

Excerpt restored by Robert Graves, The White Goddess (Graves, 2013)

Drawing Down the Moon is in all its aspects the action of invoking the goddess in her entirety into oneself. Whenever we call her into ourselves, or whenever we invoke her, we call it Drawing Down the Moon. The original ancient call has been lost, changed and rewritten so that we are only left with fragments of the original call. However, the three laws of magick are: Focus, Intention and Will. Beyond all tools, talismans and space if you have these three laws you have any ritual and magick ritual in its core essence.

The act of Drawing Down the Goddess is a spiritual state of encompassing the feminine aspect of the universe in all its magnificence. There is really no more to it except the finer details of invoking a certain aspect of her, which has only risen to popularity in modern pagan circles, calling it Drawing Down the Moon as well. The original ritualistic act was in order to bring her down in her entire form. It was not done by an unskilled practitioner due to the incredible force that the vessel or practitioner would have to withstand. The control would be paramount, and it is imperative to understand that this ritual, whether practiced as High Priestess or solitary practitioner is not for the untrained mind.

The Goddess was drawn into the practitioner so that she would be able to commune with others in the circle who could not see, hear, touch or feel her. She would only be invoked by a skilled High Priestess and the very rite of invoking her at this level was an honour of the highest magnitude.

Today, Drawing Down the Moon is practiced by anyone who has a mind to invoke the goddess. The rite itself has been watered down and it has been altered to suit the practitioner. It is common practice to be seated under the full moon and perform the ritual. The original function was to channel her essence to the people so that She could directly commune with them, today it is simply to feel her essence, or the essence of her many archetypes.

The Solitary Rite

Begin with a cleansing bath, use music and incense to allow you to enter into the frame of mind needed for sacred space. If you wish to add oils or herbs to your bath, mugwort, wormwood, sage is excellent. Alternatively, a cup of herbal tea containing mint, Vervain, mugwort, wormwood and some honey to taste is brilliant to open yourself to the art of the rite you are about to perform. (If you are pregnant do not ingest or bath with these magical herbs at all, you will cause serious harm to your unborn child.)

Remember to take a journal and pen/pencil into the circle. Writing down your thoughts once you have invoked the Goddess's wisdom which is not easily obtained beyond ritual.

Now that you are cleansed, open circle. You are allowed to wear a flowing dress, your ritual robe or go skyclad if you so wish.

Breathe deeply three times, stand with your feet shoulder apart and hold your hands, palms facing upward to the full moon and repeat this invocation:

"Ancient Mother,

Goddess above, threefold darkness and light in one,

Lover of the fiery sun,

Mother of the unknown,

Mother of the earth,

Power of the pitch black

Power of the hearth,

I call to thee,

Come to me,

Breathe in me,

Let my eyes see,

My heart believes,

Great Goddess I call to thee,

Come to me,

We are one.

Come to me,

We are one.

You are in me,

We are one."

You may now write in your journal and perform any working that you prepared. Once done, make sure to say farewell to the Goddess and close ritual space as per normal. Doing this ritual on every full moon is a fantastic way to connect with the primal feminine energy and does wonders for both male and female practitioners alike.

A Final Word of Advice from an Ol' Witch.

It is with much love that this book was written, with the added intention that you, the practitioner on this path of the wise soul, will find hope, inspiration, direction and your own voice. There are so many directions that you can go into, so many avenues for you to explore and so much that you can accomplish, and you will, if you set your mind to it.

Remember the three laws of magic, focus, will and intent, for together they are the recipe for a life of happiness and stability. Always think before you act and keep a journal or ten. Always write down everything. Collect images that you love, build a library of you. Even months after writing something, you can look back and see how you have grown. Reading and researching is a large part of the witch's path, and you do not need to have your nose in a book all the time, but one book a month is the least that you should be reading. Knowledge is indeed power. Power does not belong to the rich and famous or the ones who are influencers, it belongs to the individual, each individual. If practicing magick is your happy place, then that is the avenue you must travel.

Try as best as you can to write your own chants and your own spells. If you have the focus, the will and the intention then you cannot go wrong, and please, never harm anything for the sake of getting your way, there is no point in causing pain and nothing, but your own inner torment will come from it. Love the gods, show them gratitude and spend time in devotion and the world will be your oyster. You will know happiness like never before. Lastly, remember to love yourself, because you, dear soul, are perfect!

Merry meet, merry part, and merry meet again!

BIBLIOGRAPHY

Aelfric. (2017). *Odin's Runes: The Ancient Germanic Rune Poems.* Halldream Recordings.

Frazer, J. G. (1890). *The Golden Bough.* United Kingdom: Macmillan Publishers.

Gardner, G. B. (2009). *The Gardnerian Book of Shadows.* United States: BiblioLife.

Givens, E. (2008). *Original King James Bible.* United Kingdom: Xulon Press.

Graves, R. (2013). *The White Goddess.* New York: Farrar, Straus and Giroux.

Leland, C. G. (2018). *Aradia, or the Gospel of the Witches.* United Kingdom: Wilder Publications.

Levi, E. (1999). *The History of Magic.* United States: Weiser Books.

Mead, H. T. (2017). *The Corpus Hermeticum.* United States: Createspace Independent Publishing Platform.

Roper, L. (n.d.). *Witch Craze.* Yale University Press, New Edition (October 31, 2006).

Yurkon, G. L. (n.d.). *Gerald Brosseau Gardner.*

www.ingramcontent.com/pod-product-compliance
Lightning Source LLC
Chambersburg PA
CBHW071728080526
44588CB00013B/1935